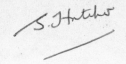 

ALL GOOD GIFTS

OWEN NANKIVELL

ALL GOOD GIFTS

A Christian View of the Affluent Society

London EPWORTH PRESS

© Owen Nankivell 1978
First published 1978
by Epworth Press
All rights reserved

No part of this publication
may be reproduced, stored in a
retrieval system, or
transmitted, in any form or by
any means, electronic, mechanical,
photocopying, recording or
otherwise, without the prior
permission of Epworth Press

7162 0305 7

Enquiries should be addressed to
The Methodist Publishing House
Wellington Road
Wimbledon
London SW19 8EU
Printed in Great Britain by
The Garden City Press Limited
Letchworth, Hertfordshire SG6 1JS

Contents

Foreword

An author does not necessarily have to give a reason for writing but I want to acknowledge two influences which have largely led to this book and to the form it has taken. A number of us in the British churches have felt for a long time, and increasingly so over the past five years, that there has been lacking in Britain any attempt by the churches to provide a sustained analysis of the many problems associated with affluence and with political economy generally. Individual Christians look to the churches for guidance in these complex areas. Society itself badly needs the injection of a properly balanced Christian view if it is to move towards desirable goals. But Christians cannot speak or act effectively, either individually or collectively, without making the attempt to achieve a proper understanding of the issues involved. The absence of anywhere where Christian resources on a sufficiently large scale were being devoted to this task led to a number of us accepting the British Council of Churches' invitation in 1973 to form a Directorate of Economic Studies under whose direction at least a start could be made to commission studies. The experience of the past five years has impressed on me even more the need for a contemporary statement of some of the basic issues facing Christians in this field and I hope what follows will help to meet this need.

Another motive behind the book is that I have become increasingly concerned that the bulk of the debate about the desirability, and justification, of the Western style of economic life and affluence has been conducted in the context of the world development problem, of the gap between rich and poor nations. I am quite prepared to accept that the strictures of Western affluence originating from that direction are justified and, as I hope I make clear in the appropriate place, the development issue presents probably the largest single issue of conscience facing Christians today. I am equally convinced, however, that a critique of Western affluence, to be comprehensive, must examine the pros and cons of the case in their own right and not simply as a derivative of a position taken up by looking at the state of the Third World. I think this more direct analysis is necessary to provide a balanced view. It is what the millions of Christians committed to, and working in, our present system have a right to expect, even if the conclusions at the end were to be the same as those arrived at by a consideration of the world development problem.

Not that I am sure the conclusions are the same. I have not set out either to attack or defend Western affluence and much of the book consists of stating the alternative viewpoints but I think it is fair to conclude from the book that I believe, by and large, that the system which has been created over the past two centuries and whose benefits we enjoy today is largely an instrument for good and a blessing of God.

The book says much about economics and theology but obviously it is not intended to be a comprehensive study of either discipline. I have included enough of each, I hope, to support the arguments of the book but I apologize to my friends who are professional economists or theologians for not satisfying their appetites in full.

My thanks go to a number of friends who have kindly read the book at various stages of drafting but, of course, leave me to take the responsibility for what is said—John Boreham, Alan Budd, Mary Douglas, Ann Harrison, Hazel Long, Amin Rajan and Kenneth Wilson—but above all to John Stacey who has had to encourage me many times to persevere and has had far more influence on what is said than he imagines.

I dedicate the book to Mary, Sally, Susan and Mark whose care for me during the dark night of authorship has been as great as their amazement that I should find economics so interesting. I also dedicate it to Bernard Jinkin who deserves answers to his questions. I hope this book will help him.

1 Introduction

This book is about a large part of modern living. Although there is much talk about our growth into maturity as humans and our freedom from our environment, from nature and from superstition, in many respects we live a life now more completely dependent than ever before in history. Our actions have never been so related to those of others or to an economic system which in turn depends for its good functioning on the acts of many thousands of individuals, in this country and around the world. We are surrounded and influenced, if not controlled, by many institutions and by rules and regulations over which we have little or at best indirect influence.

The largest single element in this set of factors is without doubt our economic environment. It is a framework which the experts, the economists and other social scientists, would like us to believe displays certain laws of behaviour so that an understanding of the system is possible in the same way as physicists provide laws concerning the physical sciences. This understanding, they claim, in turn, not only explains why things have happened in the past but also permits prediction, and therefore control, of the future. If this claim is correct, and in fact it is a highly disputable claim, then the domination over us by the economic system, and by those who control it, would be very great indeed.

The economic environment is also the stuff and matter of the daily life of most of us and it provides the main backcloth for anyone who wishes to apply principles, Christian or otherwise, to his daily life and to the search for objectives for society. Part of the task of getting back to first principles is to look at the explanations of economic behaviour offered by economists because these may be based on assumptions which make value judgements or imply views about the nature of man or the objectives of society. For example, being a social science, economics makes assumptions about the way people behave. It assumes people behave on the whole rationally and that in the main the motivation for individual behaviour is to obtain maximum satisfaction in the meeting of their individual wants. To take a specific illustration: when I buy a new suit in a shop economists assume that I have compared the prices of suits in that shop with those in other shops, that I have compared the alternative choices of spending the money on other things than a suit and that my main motivation is to give myself the pleasure (satisfaction) of having a new suit either to keep me warm, make me attractive (to whom?) or some other reason linked with self-satisfaction.

This latter point of self-satisfaction in turn raises questions concerning the economists' view of the motives and actions of individuals. Are they, are we, creatures for whom the overwhelming need is in some sense or other to meet physical wants or provide self-enjoyment? Are we at root egocentric, seeing our goals solely in terms of our own self-interest without regard to relationships? Western economics would have us place a great deal of importance on the rights and desires of the individual. In political and social terms where issues of personal liberty are involved the emphasis may have been justified and our current view of individual liberty owes a lot, perhaps, to the great wave of liberalism in the nineteenth century. As a motor force for individual living today, however, it deserves critical attention since it is possible, and indeed extremely attractive, as a means of making sense of our modern complex and interdependent society, to construct a view of personal behaviour far less individualistic and much more personal (making the distinction that the concept of person includes due regard for relationships with others) than the economist would have us assume.

Another claim of the economist that has to be critically examined is his alleged ability to make a significant contribution to social engineering; that is the task of improving society. Economists claim to understand the workings of the economy and thereby offer an ability to predict the future and, through policy measures, the means of achieving alternative goals. As the economic system pervades our everyday life so extensively, this offer is a very attractive one. It is particularly so to those, including many Christians, who strongly hope, by social change, to create a better society. The question is, however, does this claim of the economist stand up? We may fervently wish it would, but it is perhaps too much to expect from a youngish science which builds upon views about rational human behaviour. It cannot provide more than a rough guide to the consequences of the interaction of economic forces. This sober and cautious view is borne out by a brief look around us which confirms that we live in a very unstable and less than perfectly understood world. The proneness to great economic crises of our economic system which persists even today is a constant reminder of the fragility of the economist's claim. The potential of economies to malfunction is still the cause of much misery and indeed death in the poorer areas of the world. There is also a growing disenchantment in the more advanced economies where, for one reason or another, the business of achieving objectives, of keeping economic activity under control seems to be becoming more difficult.

For most Christians, this daily world of economics provides the principal set of experiences against which they have to live out their Christian principles and beliefs. They must do so with the aid of what insights they can derive either from that experience or from their particular religious convictions. However, it would be an uncritical and insensitive man who today thought that firm religious convictions in the form of generally accepted views on the nature and destiny of man and his relationship to God, in the context of the contemporary world, were to hand. For most the revolution in religious thinking and in religious practices of the past thirty years leaves little sure ground on which to take up a position. Not that this is necessarily an unwelcome situation. The emergence of the fruits of critical biblical scholarship, the development of a theology which sets the church's commitment to action squarely within the context of the secular world and the need to adopt an experiential religion, fully consistent with the humanity of man, together offer the contemporary Christian a challenge unequalled since the days of the Reformation.

One of the Christian's principal tasks is to assess the interaction between his religion and his personal involvement in the economic system. This involvement is very extensive indeed. If he adds together the time he spends in economic activity at work as part of the productive system and the time spent enjoying the fruits of the system as a consumer, the influence is seen to be all-pervasive. If that is the case he must also accept that making sense of his economic activity will to a large extent enable him to make sense of his entire life. For a Christian today the heart of the problem is to come to terms with the underlying motivation which determines both our consumption patterns and the way we are involved as producers in the system. Is it adequate to explain economic activity simply in terms of acquisitive instincts or is there underlying it something more subtle, for example, an activity concerned with making and retaining relationships and creating a sense of worth? What is certain is that economic activity must be explained in a way which permits a full understanding of our lifestyles both as it relates to the task of personal living and to the task of achieving social objectives.

A study of our modern economy cannot ignore the main economic issues facing society today. The issue of economic growth, the possibility of achieving a faster rate as well as the arguments against growth itself, is one of these. So also is the issue of the respective roles of the public and private sectors of the economy which now seems to be regarded as an acute political issue. Another question is whether the style of modern industrial society offers a full and satisfying enough opportunity for all to participate in decision-making processes. Finally, a special issue is the role of consumption in the determination of the nature and direction of economic activity generally. Consumer spending is a major influence on economic activity but it also needs to be considered in sociological terms if a proper view of why people's appetite to consume appears to have no end is to be reached.

A study of these issues could not finish without reference to the many arguments against the present affluent Western economies. Some of these arguments attack the claims of its supporters that it is the most efficient system for the provision of economic growth; others attack the basic premises underlying growth-orientated systems generally and look for alternatives.

Modern Christian living is not easy against this backcloth. Before coming to terms with the particular issues of our own economic society it is imperative on us to state where we stand on the issue of the great gap in wealth between the rich West and the poor Third World. It is a feature of Christian life to have to come to terms with situations in which the Christian is clearly failing to live up to the principles of his faith and where success has to be judged in terms of, at best, marginal achievement. The size of the world development problem, however, is so scandalous that it is difficult to see how a Western Christian can frame a programme for social improvement for his own society or justify his own life-style without making an overt and probably costly provision for reducing this gap. How the gap is to be closed is, of course, the big question.

If the flank of our attitude to world development can be held there is plenty of room for debate about the form of social advance in Britain and plenty of scope for Christian action. Perhaps the area of greatest concern for the Christian is the need to provoke balanced and fair debate at a time when the way forward in many areas is so obscure. The Christian, whether individually or through the church, must find the appropriate way of contributing to this debate while always retaining the right to stand in judgement of society if necessary.

The Christian also has to mould his own life-style out of the complex economic system around him. It is not an easy task and it is probably fair to say that the church's teaching is steadily becoming irrelevant to some of the main issues facing the Christian today. An example of this is to be found in the teaching of the church about work itself. Since biblical times until very recently (and still so in most of the world) in most cultures man's daily task has been self-evident. It has been to work for food, clothing and shelter in order to keep alive. Even when some margin has been possible it has been used to make life that bit easier within the context of a life largely devoted to economic activity.

Even if the attempt is made it is very hard to translate these early concepts into terms which relate to the fabric of the modern industrial economy. There is an enormous momentum of religious thinking that still attempts to persuade us to assume that the work ethic remains the central thought around which we judge ourselves and justify our patterns of life. This is so despite the fact that so often the industrial complex in which we find ourselves offers no comparable satisfaction of a job well done and despite the fact that most of us in the West have long since passed the point where daily labour is solely devoted to giving us food, clothing and shelter. Maybe what is wanted now is a leisure ethic, but most certainly Christians have an enormous task ahead of them if they are to make sense of behaviour and actions much more orientated to pleasures derived from consumption patterns far removed from essentials and in a context of far more leisure time. It is a crisis of motivation and objectives which is felt strongly by the modern Christian and on which he gets little help from tradition or from a contemporary understanding of the Christian faith.

Another example where the church's teaching is lacking is the Christian's attitude to consumption. By and large consumption has been regarded simply in terms of a satisfaction of appetite and greed. It therefore comes in for considerable knocking from Christian moralists, especially those concerned with the development issue. It may be that appetite and greed are the dominant forces behind our consumer society in which case we stand very much under judgement. The probability, however, is that motives are more complicated than that and that the underlying frenzied passion for consumption reflects an effort to build or maintain an intricate web of inter-relationships and methods of communication, affecting the individual's sense of worth—issues of equal concern of the Christian.

The Christian's need to relate his theology to his daily life goes deeper still since he now feels obliged to identify himself fully as a Christian with secular activity. The consequences of the development in the church's teaching about the relevance of lay experience, which began with Luther's teaching of the sanctity of daily work, have now arrived with full force to the point where the Christian feels he can only adopt an understanding of life, activity and relationships which, at all times and in all respects, is consistent with his basic humanity. He regards himself primarily as a human being, a member of mankind, and cannot therefore interpret his position in any way which detracts from that fact.

This stance means that the Christian must look for his encounter with God within each and every human situation. He must believe in a way more relevant today than ever before in the fact that 'the earth is the Lord's and the fullness thereof': which means that he must acknowledge the working of God in every part of our great complex, secular and humanistic socio-economic system. This is the challenge given to us by modern theological insights—that we have to recognize that we are grounded in the secular and it is there that we encounter God.

This encounter with God may often involve taking a stand on moral issues stemming from the Christian's understanding of love, neighbourliness, stewardship and justice and may often result in the need for action both in terms of personal relationships and in the context of social planning. But it has to be asked whether such action is a sufficient response to God's demands, whether or not there is a higher definition of the relationship between men and God which rests simply on God's will that we should be obedient to him?

We must now set about the rather formidable task of answering these questions in more detail. The next three chapters construct a framework for the rest of the book by considering in turn aspects of economics and the modern economy as they bear on Christian views of the individual and society, some relevant elements in the current theological debate and finally an examination of the layman's field of experience and particularly the implication of the 'compromised' situation for Christian living.

That section is followed by two chapters developing particular issues in contemporary economic and industrial society and particularly the consumer goods society on which a Christian trying to make sense of our affluent society must have a judgement. This, however, is followed by a chapter acknowledging the various bodies of opinion which reject, in part, or in whole, the Western style of affluence.

After a chapter bringing the themes together, the final section of the book outlines a position on which it is possible to base a Christian view of the affluent society; first, in the world development context, secondly in our social and political life and finally in terms of the individual Christian lifestyle.

2 Preliminary thoughts—on economics

What economics is about

There is no simple description of what economics is about, even though all of us have a commonsense awareness, based on our daily lives, of the scope of the subject. The difficulty arises when an attempt to give precision to the definition is made. One approach, however, is to describe its techniques and methods. Economics is, for example, very much concerned with making the best use of resources available. The ability to produce goods is, at any one time, strictly limited by the availability of supplies of factors of production, that is to say, materials, the size of the labour force and its skills and the quality of management and the size and quality of the stock of capital of machines, etc. Our ability to satisfy our wants and demands is, as a result, also limited. The question is, therefore, how to make the best use of what we have to meet limited objectives; a concern for efficiency and optimization. These criteria are usually applied to market situations. A market is a place (although it does not have to have a geographical location) where the strength of supply and demand for a product or a factor of production is tested and brought into balance via a pricing mechanism. This will usually be done by the setting of a price which will clear the market in the sense that at that price the amount being offered for sale will equal the amount being demanded.

There are, of course, many different markets and the listing of a number of them will serve better than anything to illustrate the content of economics. For example, economists are interested in what determines the demand for a particular product such as an item of food or a suit of clothes. This has led them to formulate theories explaining the way in which demand responds to changes in prices and has given rise to a very large area of interest: the theory of consumer behaviour.

Similarly on the supply side the problem of how firms react to price changes has led to the study of the theory of the firm. How does an individual firm decide how much to produce of what products and at what price? How does it balance up the cost and revenue consequences of its production decisions?

Another market is that in which the supply of and demand for labour is brought into balance. The demand for labour is closely related to the production decisions of individual firms. The supply of labour is affected by many factors not all of which are strictly economic but they do include the availability of different types of labour with different types of skills. The price here, of course, is the level of wages.

To take a final example, economists are concerned with the way in which countries themselves trade with each other (a market situation with an international dimension) and especially with the ways in which the relative prices of internationally traded goods are reconciled by the exchange rate mechanism.

These examples illustrate the primary interest of the economist in the different market/pricing mechanisms which make up our everyday economic life, and go a long way—but, of course, not the whole way—to describe what economics is all about.

The economist has always looked beyond the study of individual markets. They are, of course, important, but they are also interdependent and taken together they make up a system which requires to be studied in its own right. It is a system in the sense that a series of inter-related sets of causal relationships can be brought together and used not only to influence individual market situations but to control the system itself as a whole. The inter-relationship of individual markets is often obvious. The demand for suits is determined by the price of suits relative to the prices of other consumer goods. That demand will determine the quantity of suits produced and the wages of those working in the suit-making industry. The price of the suits relative to the price of suits made abroad will affect exports and imports and, therefore, domestic production as well. From the early days of economics, however, as far back as the Physiocrats, the early French school of economists (see, for example, Quesnay's Tableau Economique), attention has been given to the characteristics of the system as a whole. This area of macro-economics[1] has attracted particular interest since the Second World War largely because the theoretical developments in economics in the post-war period were heavily influenced by a reaction to the great slump in the world economy in the 1930s; a time when the traditional economist view of the workings of individual markets, whether of goods, labour or currencies, seemed unable to indicate the appropriate adjustment mechanisms required to stimulate recovery.

The contribution of Keynes
It was this situation of the 1930s and particularly the intolerably high and chronic levels of unemployment that led to the emergence of perhaps the largest single contribution to economic analysis since

[1] As distinct from micro-economics—the study of individual markets.

the discipline was founded—the General Theory of Employment of John Maynard Keynes.[2] Keynes' contention was that the mainstream view of economics—that there was a self-balancing mechanism inherent in the pricing system both for goods and for labour which would ensure that markets were cleared and that there could be no permanent unemployment—was falsified by the chronic unemployment of that time. He proposed the alternative view that there was no reason why an equilibrium situation should not arise in which there was less than full employment. His argument was based mainly on the proposition that two main components of demand, investment and, to a lesser extent, private consumption were determined largely by psychological factors—the future expected return on risk capital in the former case and the desire to save in the latter. If these factors were depressed no matter how much prices reacted (consumer good prices, interest rates or wage rates) it was quite possible for the amount of effective demand to be less than was required to maintain full employment. In the circumstances Keynes' prescription was the use of public expenditure to generate the required extra demand which would not only take up the slack but also improve confidence to the point where investment and personal consumption would recover and play their part in maintaining full employment.

Anyone trained in economics in this country since the war and perhaps up to, say, five years ago will have grown up under the influence of this Keynesian system. Published in 1936, the General Theory was soon to achieve a dominant place in post-war theory and practice. Most developments of economic theories since the Second World War have taken the form of filling in, explaining and justifying different aspects of the General Theory. This is not the place to provide a detailed critique of Keynesian thinking but the domination of the theory cannot be stressed too strongly. It has been accepted almost universally since it offered the most complete and, to many, the most satisfactory explanation of the reason for the depression in the mid-war years by explaining the inherent cyclical nature of the capitalist economies and appeared to offer the technical means for ensuring such a situation could not arise again.

It has also been extremely influential in its effect on practical policies. It has, as a theoretical system, underpinned most aspects of Western economic policy and practice. It has been the essential tool for demand management, i.e. the control of the economy to achieve full employment by influencing aggregate demand. It has also been

[2] John Maynard Keynes, *The General Theory of Employment, Interest and Money*, Macmillan 1936.

the basis of the type of longer term planning such as has prevailed in Western Europe since the end of the war and has also provided the framework for the attack on the problem of development in the Third World. It would not be an exaggeration to call the system the essential tool of the practising social democrat, i.e. the prevalent Western style of government since the end of the war.

The current influence of the Keynesian system needs to be stressed because despite the emergence of rival theories and the current attacks on it, it has dominated the scene for the past forty years and a full recognition of the contribution of the system is required in order to understand what modern economics is about. It is a system that claims to show how economic activity at large is determined and concerns itself with the determination of the total level of demand, output and employment. It therefore makes large claims which are of vital importance to each member of society. Derivable from this general claim are two subsidiary claims which are important to the current study. The first is the offer of a scientific system explaining how the economy works and the second is the offer of hope of being able to change the course of events and thereby achieve predetermined objectives. This claim to be scientific and successful is a very large one and should it be proved false would be a serious blow to those wishing to change or improve society since the achievement of economic objectives is by far the main task facing social engineers.

The claims of economics
Like any other member of society the Christian must come to terms with this system which affects almost all his daily life in one respect or another. While he cannot claim or wish to understand economics in all its complexity he has a right to have pointed out the basic underlying propositions so that he can assess how they bear on his understanding of society and on his own nature and destiny.

Western economics is based, not entirely but largely, upon the concept of a market in which the wishes of the individual consumer are paramount. As will be shown later the validity of this assumption has to be qualified very heavily but the underlying principle of the market is clear: that of consumer sovereignty. The economist does not claim to philosophize or to moralize about the concept of individualism but the need for individuals to be able to express their choice in a rational manner and satisfy their needs underpins a large part of economic theory. When the economy is looked at from a point of view of our involvement in the production process, rather than from the point of view of consumption, the influence of individualism is less obvious but nevertheless much of the theory of wage determination and the distribution of factor incomes is based on a similar view of individualism and the satisfaction of basic acquisitive needs in terms of reward and ambition.

A similar issue arises over the concept of optimization. Economics is about the use of scarce resources to achieve a number of competing objectives and is thus concerned from first to last with the efficient or optimum use of resources. The development of techniques allowing analysis in this way is an extremely valuable contribution to the task of improving society and in concept is very close to the principle of stewardship with which the general Christian reader will be familiar. Although, however, the economist makes much of the efficient allocation of resources he remains essentially neutral, in an ethical or normative sense, about the actual use to which particular resources are put. He will often ask for an objective function against which to work; that is to say a set of indicators showing the importance of achieving individual objectives relative to each other, for example, the trade-off between improving the balance of payments surplus by, say, £500 million and reducing the level of unemployment by, say, 500,000 or increasing the rate of inflation by 1 per cent per annum. What he will not do, however, is lay claim to the task of setting this objective function; that is the task of the politician and society in general. Economics is concerned with identifying what is wanted by society, and with the search for the best way of meeting those wants at minimum cost. For example, if an economist is studying the market for television sets he will try to measure the strength of demand for sets at different prices and the likely supply of sets that will be forthcoming at each price. He will also be prepared to assess whether there is any hindrance or malfunctioning in the market which prevents competitive pressures ensuring the optimum price is achieved. What he will not do is make value judgements on whether people should be buying more television sets rather than, for example, spending it on 'something better' or paying the money in taxes in the interest of a public project or transferring his purchasing power to fellow humans in the Third World.[3]

Most Western economists believe very firmly that a pricing mechanism operating through a free market is the most efficient means of achieving the best use of economic resources. This view is largely shared by economists of all persuasions regardless of the

[3] Welfare economics, a branch of economics, gets closest to passing judgement on alternative uses but only in a limited technical sense and not in the more general sense referred to here.

political wing to which they are attracted. There are other countries in the world where things are run differently and where the allocation is in some sense determined by public will and there are ways of ensuring an optimal use of resources in this fashion, but few Western economists have seriously argued that the West should experiment substantially in this way. This is not to say that there are not imperfections, and in some cases rather substantial imperfections, in a market system, and these will be discussed in later chapters, but the proposition being made here is simply that the Western economist in seeking to achieve an efficient use of resources is strongly convinced that the price mechanism, whereby people wanting goods and those supplying goods can conveniently and efficiently reveal their respective wants and preferences, appears to be the most practical system to adopt as the basic framework. If it is departed from, the task of guaranteeing an efficient allocation of resources becomes much more difficult.

To complement theories explaining the market for goods, economists have constructed a similar set of propositions to explain how rewards to the various factors of production, for example, labour, capital and land are determined. Here again, to the economist, the main criterion is the search for a system which is efficient, i.e. which effectively ensures that people or machines are in the right place and in sufficient quantity at the right time to meet given demands. A firm, for example, in determining its production plans will take into account not only the revenue to be earned at different levels of production, but also the varying costs of producing different amounts. Included in the latter costs are, for example, the firm's labour costs. The firm thus has a demand for labour determined by the market for its good and by the price of labour (i.e. the level of wages); and the labour force, in a sense, is supplying labour at a price. As will be seen later, many qualifications have to be attached to this simple statement of the determination of the reward to labour but the economist primarily sees the problem as the determination, via a market, of a balance between supply and demand through the operation of a pricing mechanism. In this area, even more perhaps than in the case of the demand for products, the economist wishes to stress his neutrality on the normative aspects of relative rewards. The present system results, for example, in a disc jockey earning very large amounts because of the teenage demand for his specialist services. While many may be distressed by the gap in income and wealth between such a disc jockey and, for example, a more pedestrian shop foreman in a declining heavy engineering industry, the foreman's wage packet is determined essentially in similar fashion. Labour and capital have, as it were, an offer price and they will be employed where the remuneration is best which in turn will be in areas where the demand is strongest or labour is in shortest supply.

The problem of growth and full employment

A feature of post-war economics has been a belief in an ability to plan for growth. The idea of economic growth as something that can be planned for and controlled is mainly of recent origin. Hard on the publication of Keynes' General Theory theoretical schools adopting the theory developed it to explain the mechanics by which economies grow over time and thus offered the means whereby the community could plan for a faster rate of growth if it is so desired. In the last two decades the achievement of faster growth rates has become a sensitive and important political objective.[4]

It is doubtful whether economists would be so confident now (in the late 1970s) in their ability to prescribe the means to create faster growth. One indication of weakness in the ability of the theory to do so has emerged in the field of development economics where Western economic advice to developing countries to enable them to imitate Western growth has not been overblessed with success. A more substantial body-blow, however, has been delivered in recent years, particularly in Britain where there has been a persistent failure to identify the changes required in order to accelerate the rate of growth; culminating in the depression of 1975–6 when unemployment levels rose back to the highest levels since the 1930s—the problem to which Keynes originally addressed himself.

The objective of the maintenance of full employment is central to modern economic policy. The Keynesian theory itself arose out of the shambles of the inter-war years when it seemed that there was no way in which jobs could be created for all who required them or any way in which the appalling pool of unemployment could be reduced. Almost all economists now accept that a main criterion of the efficiency of the economic machine is whether it is able to create sufficient sustained work for the mass of the working population. This is, of course, as much a social as an economic objective. Despite the limited success in controlling the level of demand in recent

[4] The objective was pursued successfully in Continental Europe during the 1950s and moved into the centre of British economic policy early in the 1960s where it has remained since. The increased emphasis on growth is largely a result of the increased awareness of the contribution of faster growth to the provision of better public services and a higher standard of living.

years, most economists would still claim sufficient understanding of the way in which the economic system creates more or less jobs and what needs to be done to maintain a satisfactory level of employment. Success in this area is certainly crucial to the role of the economist since unless he can perform well here he will be under great criticism. It has always been recognized, however, that some amount of unemployment is inevitable. There are always a number of people who for one reason or another are unemployable. There will always be some, at any one time, who are in the process of changing from one job to another as a result of choice or because of some structural change in industry. The level also fluctuates with the trade cycle, being higher when activity is depressed and lower when activity is higher. This latter variation simply reflects the inability to smooth out the vagaries of the trade cycle and in an ideal world the economy would be so controlled that unemployment was kept steady and at a minimum level. But what constitutes a minimum level is a matter of controversy amongst economists and cannot be separated from other issues such as the causes of inflation.

Economics is about people

Whatever the merits of the different views about the level and significance of unemployment economists do well to remember that not only is this a key area in which the relevance and effectiveness of their theories is put to the test but it is an area which drives home the point that for all its sophistication and abstraction economic theory is, in the end, about people. This latter point is one on which economists are somewhat sensitive. They realize that behind terms such as the pressure of demand or the weakness of the labour market lies the tragedy of people wanting work but not being able to find it and they appreciate that it suggests that the economist can be accused of not caring about people; of being only concerned with a mechanistic, impersonal and often apparently ruthless system. Most economists would want to challenge this view of the profession. They would lay claim to a great concern about people and for the search for solutions which will improve people's economic circumstances. The point about the concern of the economist is that he regards the solution to many problems which have personal implications such as poverty, the inability to find work, is to be found at an aggregate or a national level. Hence his concern is for the economy as a whole, but it is none the less personally orientated in that the end result is the well-being of the individuals making up the system. The economist would not want to claim special understanding or a more important role than others, but he has a right to object to criticism that he is not as interested in personal well-being as others.

Economics and politics

The economist is half-brother to the politician and indeed observers may be forgiven for often confusing the two roles when a great deal of political activity is concerned with the achievement of economic objectives.[5] The economist, as we have seen, regards himself as one who seeks to understand how the economic system works and hopes thereby to contribute an analysis of how things happen and what the consequences will be by following certain lines of policy. He does not regard it as his function to take political decisions any more than to make value judgements. This sense of neutrality is professed constantly but it can be argued that economists have been less than convincing in persuading others of their objectivity. This is partly because they are invariably involved in politics in practical terms. But it is also because many people doubt that in the last resort economics is a neutral science since it is based on propositions about human behaviour. Inevitably, therefore, the economist is caught up in the ebb and flow of people's attitudes about the economic environment and their view of the objectives for economic policy. Whether he likes it or not his business will be associated and linked in the minds of most with the political attempts to achieve economic objectives. He may not like this politicizing of his task, but he would be unwise to pretend it did not exist. In fact, he would be a poor and limited economist if he tried to free himself entirely from the association.

The contribution to social engineering

Most economists have assumed that the economic system they are examining and seeking to control is, in fact, controllable; that the thousands of individual decisions making up economic activity contrive to produce a stable result. There are some economists who believe that the economy in a 'natural state' is convergent, that is to say, a divergent process such as an inflationary tendency or a bad harvest will be self-correcting by setting up somewhere else in the system a compensating process bringing it under control and back to stability. More realistically most economists will accept that there are many destabilizing factors at work in the world such as wars, droughts, unpredictable behaviour by certain parts of the system

[5] For a long period the discipline was called political economy, a more apt name in many respects.

which if uncontrolled could lead to ultimate disaster and ruin but argue that the economist offers tools, through his views of the way the economy works, for controlling the effects of these changes and bringing the economy either at national or world level back into control. There are many who now would feel that this belief in a natural or contrived ability to convergence is a somewhat optimistic assumption.

The limitations of economics

However well economics is regarded economists would be the first to admit its many limitations. Some of these are obvious even to the most superficial observer. Others are much less obvious and some are hidden to the extent that even economists themselves are barely aware of them. Like all disciplines its practitioners are often influenced by the thinking of their age and have to be judged within that constraint.

(a) Economic factors alone One of the more obvious sins of omission confessed by economists is the limitation of their analysis to economic factors alone. They recognize the pervading influence of non-economic factors in many areas of their studies. To take one important example: most economic models[6] in seeking to explain consumer demand relate demand for particular goods to relative prices, to income and wealth and to savings habits. It is possible to 'explain' the level of savings in terms of building up wealth or as a precaution against a rainy day, but it is an element which is extremely sensitive to people's psychological attitudes such as their degree of confidence in the way the economy is being run or, more personally, their judgement of the security of their own job. The way people react in this respect can have a crucial bearing on the level of demand and economists would never wish to claim that his 'model' for explaining consumer behaviour will be adequate at all times. He would certainly admit at a time of economic crisis he was in the domain of the social psychologist rather than the economist and would voluntary impose restraints upon the value of his own modelling which is unable to build such attitudes easily into a cause and effect relationship. Nor can the economist generally take into account the effect on issues like economic growth, and performance, of human attitudes on the factory floor such as boredom from doing monotonous jobs and other non-economic social attitudes in contemporary Western economies. Nor can the economist make much sense of the saints, prophets and cranks of

[6] The term 'model' is used here and elsewhere to mean a set of causal relationships designed to explain a particular economic phenomenon.

this world who behave in economically irrational ways by refusing to have wants to satisfy, by refusing to be rewarded for effort in the same way as their fellow men and by absurdly giving much of what they earn away.

(b) Social consequences of economic activity The economist is also somewhat at a loss to know how to deal with the social as distinct from the private consequences of economic activity. Although a market system free of friction can maximize personal satisfaction, it may in the process produce undesirable social effects. For example, an efficient firm producing goods clearly demanded by the market may, in the process of producing them, spoil the atmosphere, pollute rivers and generate all sorts of socially undesirable consequences. Equally other firms or individuals may put at risk the safety of their workmates or members of the community at large. Or firms may use public resources, such as roads, for private gain without paying the full social cost for their use. Attempts can be made to take these factors into account without losing the benefits of the market system, for example, by changing prices artificially through taxation, to make people pay the full social cost of what they are doing, or to make sure benefits fall to society rather than to individuals. But economics has for too long regarded these as incidental extras, as it were, to their system and the time perhaps has been reached when society in general is inclined to give them greater priority and much more weight. Society had probably, rightly, identified that the weakness of the economic system in this respect is its slowness of response. There is an uncomfortable feeling, for example, that pollution can gain a firm grip long before the market economy is aware of it and the price mechanism can be made to work to reduce or remove its effect.

(c) The implied value judgements. For all the economist's claim to neutrality and objectivity it is not difficult to find, just below the surface, basic philosophical premises in his system which are by no means undisputed by people today. A great deal of economic thought is based on what may be called a nineteenth-century liberalism with an especially heavy emphasis on individualism. This shows itself in many ways, including both the economist's view that the nub of the system is a market acting as a clearing house between a multitude of individuals and a theory of consumption (central to the whole system) which is based on the proposition that what the individual does is best. Collectivism as an efficient means of revealing and satisfying choice is frowned upon and the regard of people as persons with responsibilities for their social consequences (in contrast to individualism) is played down. This set of assumptions,

whether they are intended or not, leads economists towards a position which, in the interests of efficiency, has a built-in resistance to most sorts of intervention, against protectionism in its widest sense and in favour wherever possible of a *laissez-faire* approach. Even those economists who support intervention appear to regard it as a regrettable necessity brought in only to adjust a malfunctioning marketing system. This does not mean, of course, that economists are not concerned about issues like income inequalities and the position of the poor. What it does mean, however, is that most prefer to seek to achieve social objectives in such areas by measures which have the minimal effect on the free working of the market economy such as the redistribution of incomes by taxation and social benefits rather than by predetermining earned incomes.

Postscript

As a postscript to this chapter two thoughts, one optimistic and one pessimistic, need to be expressed and they both relate essentially to the current state of the discipline and bear particularly on the search for solutions to get the Western economies out of their present economic predicament. The first, the optimistic one, is that in recent years there has been a development in economics which offers at least the prospect of a substantial improvement in the ability to understand the workings of the economy. This development is the emergence of the techniques of econometric modelling as a tool for economists to use in helping in formulating and implementing economic policy. Traditionally, economics has been a mixture of a spartan theoretical approach, a close neighbour to mathematical logic, in which efforts have been directed to distilling the basic elements of the economic process. However useful this tool has been in expressing the underlying logic of economics, it leaves a great deal to be desired in terms of understanding the real world.

There has, however, always been a strong section of economists who have retained a shrewd sense of observation about real life. Some thirty years ago this interest in observing what was actually going on and the attempts to quantify and examine empirically the basic propositions of economics took on an added dimension and force with the emergence of the separate study of econometrics.[7] Since then a systematic attempt has been made to apply statistical and other estimation techniques to data on a large scale about the real world in order to see whether the basic propositions in economics could be validated or not. Such developments have, however, hitherto been limited by two constraints. The first was the

[7] Literally, the science of measurement in economics.

absence of a data base of consistent data stretching over many years against which theories could be tested and the second was the absence of computer power to enable the models constructed by the economists to be fitted and tested.

Although the use of this type of modelling has not had a great deal of success in recent years, to do it justice, it is still in its infancy and the main fruits to be gained from the work are yet to come. If it were to succeed as its supporters believe it will, a new stage in social engineering will be opened up.[8]

The pessimistic thought is simply to reflect on the experience of the last few years and to draw attention to the sense of frustration and pessimism shared by economists today in the poor performance of their theories in the face of the economic storms around them; particularly since the rise in oil prices in late 1973. To take two examples amongst many. First, very few economists in the late 1960s would have ever expected that inflation would have accelerated as unemployment rose during 1970 and 1971. Up to that time the conventional wisdom was that these two factors could be traded off one against the other. The second example is that very few economists in the 1960s would have foreseen the size of the secondary effects, and their consequences for internal inflation, of the decision to devalue the pound in 1967 and the later floating of the exchange rate from the early 1970s. Both these examples of the early 1970s exposed cruelly the current limitations of economics. Their consequences have been quite dramatic and have thrown the economic community into great disarray. This disarray can only be regarded as a tragedy at a time when economic problems are so acute and when a sense of crisis is felt by all sections of society.

The view of economics since the war is thus one of a mixture of both hope and gloom, of the strength of a young discipline with a great deal to offer society as it moves forward, yet in some senses is one that is crucially constrained by its own history and environment out of which it has grown. It has much to answer for, both good and bad, and is crucially linked to the concepts of growth, wealth and materialism, all elements of social development which are increasingly being questioned by society at large.

Of all the points raised in this chapter three perhaps deserve special mention and re-emphasis before we go on to develop the larger theme of this book. The first is to recognize the pervasiveness of economics. Our lives are to a very large part orientated around and

---

[8] If, for example, economists were to reach the point where they had the same degree of understanding and control of the economy as control engineers appear to have in monitoring and controlling industrial production.

determined by the system of production and consumption. We spend most of our active life participating in it in one way or another. Life consists to a great extent of enjoying the fruits of that activity and most of our relationships with others and our own sense of worth is revealed and given meaning by, and through, the materialistic culture. If we, therefore, believe to any extent at all in an experiential faith, that is to say a faith that only finds complete meaning and relevance in the daily experience of life, then it is clear that much of the task of living, in the sense of discovering and practising faith, will, in this day and age, take place within the economic system itself. Relationships with others will be with fellow workers either directly, for example on the shop floor, or indirectly through friends who share the same economic and industrial experience. The sense of God's purpose will have to be seen as much in terms of the ultimate destination of our affluent society as in terms of nature and the traditional pre-industrial life. There is therefore no backing away for the Christian, he had no choice but to come to terms with the environment in which he has been placed.

The second point relates to the role of the economist himself. People in general are content to live with scientific systems and on the whole trust the practitioner. We mainly take for granted the network of electricity in towns, the transport system, town planning and can usually safely work on the assumption that people who devised these things knew what they were doing and are able to keep the systems in control. There is a tendency to do the same for economics. The economists, we assume, understand the problems of economies as engineers understand the problems of bridge-building are expected to be as successful in social engineering as engineers are in civil engineering. We have a trust of the expert in this field as in others. In the case of economics this trust is doubly important because economics is about human welfare, in a far more intimate sense than, say, in engineering. Moreover, not only is it more sensitive in this sense, but economics appeals to all who look forward to steady progress towards a better world. The claim of the economist to understand and therefore to control and direct the economy is crucial to the social engineer seeking to improve society and vital to Christians who have a special concern to 'grow not weary in well-doing'. It matters vitally whether the economist's claim to be able to do these things is true or false and regrettably experience of the last ten years has served to throw considerable doubt upon this claim.

Finally, to repeat, economics, unlike the natural sciences, is ultimately about people and the Christian has, therefore, to take an interest in what precise view of the nature of man is being subsumed by the economist. Not only may it be one that is contrary to his own view as a Christian but because of the pervasiveness of the economic system it may be that the economist's view, whatever it may be, is so built into the system that constraints are imposed which prevent or hinder the development of a true Christian view. There are undoubtedly grounds for concern. As has been pointed out, underlying economics is an individualistic view of man which condition views about what the true purpose of the economic system should be; for example, the maximization of personal welfare, or the preservation of the market place in which individual needs can best be revealed. The difficulties with this approach, from a Christian point of view, are that while it pays great recognition to personal liberty it may not enable the concept of people as persons, that is with an obligation to build social relationships and accept social responsibilities, to be developed adequately. Moreover, it may well, as later chapters will suggest, lead to a bias towards private activities against public and social decisions which the Christian would find difficult to accept.

There are, also, other ways in which the Christian is bound to relate economics to his understanding of his Christian position, i.e. his theology, and we must now turn to an examination of the contemporary theological view in so far as it bears on economics.

3 Preliminary thoughts—on theology

A time of change

Christians who have grown up since the war, have followed the various theological developments and have been involved in the changing patterns of church institutions and religious attitudes have experienced an almost unceasing onslaught on their traditional beliefs and most of their practices. There have been other ages when Christ's flock have felt challenged and under threat but it is doubtful whether the totality of the threat has ever been as great as it has been and still remains in our present time.

Not all of this threat can be regarded as bad and detrimental. The Christian has no claim to a quiet life, free from doubt and oppression, nor can he bank on the earthly comforts of popularity and approbation that have emerged from time to time when religion has become fashionable. History suggests that on the whole the Christian must expect difficult times; it also seems to suggest that the rough times are the better ones for the Christian. Be that as it may, each one of us has no option in the matter since we are placed in our own situation and must in some way or other come to terms with it. Contemplation on the more favoured situation of others in other countries, or of other generations, may comfort a little but will not change the task facing us.

(a) The churches in decline One of the threatening changes to the Christian has been the decline in church membership. Christians are not supposed to be concerned about numbers. It is recorded that Jesus said 'Where two or three are gathered in my name' not 'two or three thousand'. Church leaders (and for that matter the man in the pew) therefore always feel rather guilty when reacting adversely to statistics of church membership or other indicators of the decline in the practice of religion. That decline, however, is very real and the contemporary Christian must adjust to it, if not with regret then at least realistically because it must be built into his planning assumptions upon which he expects to conduct his life or contribute to the work of the church.

The facts themselves are self-evident. Almost all branches of the British Christian community have shown substantial decline in church membership, adherence or practice since the war. For the Methodist Church the figure of total membership stood at 750,000 in 1946; the comparable figure for 1975 was 450,000. Other churches show a similar decline: the only areas of growth at the moment appear to be the Evangelical and Pentecostal movements.

This decline in membership must mean something though it cannot be assumed that it implies an equivalent loss of faith. There are many other reasons why people might decide not to continue attending a church or not to declare their allegiance by accepting membership and its obligations. There is a strong case for believing that most of our decline has been secular in the sense that it reflects changes in social or sociological habits rather than any weakening of faith. However the term 'weakening of faith' is itself ambiguous and while many non-church-goers may say that they continue to believe in God they will describe so blurred a concept that it is no comfort at all to a committed Christian. On the other hand, many people have ceased to go to church either because they have found far more attractive pursuits, such as watching colour television, or because they have become so utterly bored with church attendance that they see no point in going on. The proper reaction to this situation on the part of the churches is an issue which goes outside the terms of reference of this book. What is relevant is that this reduction in church attendance and religious practice presents a depressing backcloth which affects the attitudes adopted by practising Christians to their lifestyle and to their contribution to society in general. The fact is that many Christians today began their Christian adult lives in full churches, where the act of corporate worship, through strength of numbers alone, provided a spiritual uplift and where the attendance at church and at its functions engendered an air of confidence which spilled over into the daily life of the committed Christian. The size of today's congregations is a constant reminder of the fact that those days have passed, at least for the time being, and no amount of rationalizing and reformulation of the theories of the nature of worship can close the eyes to the empty pews and the scanty singing.

An even more substantial consequence of the decline, which is by no means entirely unwelcome, is the realization that committed Christians are very much in a minority in society and they must therefore know clearly why they are taking up a stand as Christians. Christians, of course, have always been a minority but, as long as the community played such overt lip service to Christian values as it has, at least for the past two centuries, and as long as declared Christians were relatively plentiful in numbers, even though a minority, the individual Christian was shielded from some of the sterner realities of the consequences and implications of his faith. It was no great witness to stand up to defend the Christian virtues if society in general had accepted them as its own. Nowadays it is quite clear that in many respects society is adopting other standards (or at least discarding old ones) and Christians are increasingly finding that the taking of a Christian view is seen as a greater act of commitment.[1]

Individual Christians are thus feeling increasingly exposed. It is now something of significance to declare oneself a Christian since it represents, or it should represent, an acceptance of a style of life and an adherence to principles and belief in ultimates, which are almost certainly not likely to be shared by companions at work or in social recreation. The achievement of this sense of identity which, of course, must not develop into bigotry or self-gratification, is the stuff of which real Christians are made and forged.

The disappearance of the familiar landmarks of church adherence, of security within a minority group that nevertheless had achieved some sort of recognition and place in the secular society, has meant that the Christian had had to reconsider the context in which he has had to develop and live out his Christian faith. Events in fact leave him no choice if he is to retain any sort of reality to the nature of Christian witness and experience. Christian has to be grounded henceforth in daily life and in the secular situation. It is no longer a question of, as it were, moving out of church into the world to witness and apply Christian principles—such imagery in any case always carried a scandal of dualism quite contrary to Christian teaching—but instead it is a question of accepting that the secular experience itself is the arena for encountering God. Our humanism becomes the grounds for practising true religion and becomes our strength and not our weakness. To many of us this realization that, regretful as the breakdown of conventional religious practices may be, they only serve to point us to the real stuff of religious experience, has redeemed a situation which otherwise would have appeared lost.

(b) The impact of modern theology. This book is not a theological study and will not attempt a comprehensive description of the various theological schools that have influenced recent generations. But the point has to be made that the average Christian has had to come to terms with quite massive changes in the understanding of the relationships between man and his God and man and creation. These are not necessarily recent insights, most of the theological views that have gained strength and have caused so much controversy in recent years were, in fact, formulated by theologians well

[1] This observation is not intended to be a condemnation of recent relaxations in codes of morality, many of which are to be welcomed; the point is simply being made that Christians are increasingly feeling that their stand identifies them as such and therefore their commitment has to be that more conscious.

before the Second World War. Their arrival on the scene, however, has been none the less dramatic for the delay in coming and each of us must make his own choice amongst the various reformulations and restatements on offer.

There are many people who continue to hold on to the basic position that the Bible is composed of literal and eternal truths but for others the insight into the background of the New Testament writings provided by contemporary theologians[2] has led to a quite radical revision of our understanding of what those writings are trying to say. Such researches, clearly carried out honestly and open-mindedly in the best intellectual traditions of biblical scholarship, provide a serious attempt to recognize what can be regarded as literally true and what is there by way of enrichment, as an oral tradition was converted into a written one, or by way of theological overtones imposed by the early church. Those of us who have accepted the consequences of this biblical scholarship do not in any way feel a sense of loss in doing so; rather a sense of liberation and excitement about the journey that opens up before us as we begin to pursue the paths suggested by this scholarship.

Perhaps the most important consequence is the recognition that it is necessary to get beyond the alleged historical facts in order to understand the religious implications of critical parts of the Bible, especially those relating to the life and nature of Christ. This means interpreting the narrative of the Bible in a way that, through its historical context, it can be seen to be fully relevant to the situation of today. It also means abandoning the position of an objective reader and, instead, participating in the experience of comprehending the message in an active, committed searching way, being in a sense a contemporary party to the action. This position, which is essentially an existential view of belief, is one of the challenging theological contributions of the past two or three decades, even though it is exposed to the accusation of relativity and subjectivity in contrast to the allegedly more objective position of the traditional view.

A consequence of adopting this existential point of view is that it gives encouragement to Christians who are sensitive to their humanity, and wish to interpret their lives in humanistic terms in the sense of seeing religion as an integral part of making sense of everday experience. By so doing the Christian is able to ground his beliefs in his basic human experience, thereby being really true to himself and able to respect his humanity. Both his desire to worship and serve God and his obligation to serve his fellow men can then be worked

[2] For example, the writings of Rudolph Bultman, *Primitive Christianity*, 1956, and *Jesus and the Word*, 1934, Fontana Books.

out in terms of a comprehensive devotion to God. He is also encouraged to identity himself with his fellow men so that, regardless of whether he is with believers or not, he can still display his humanity and identify himself in, and commit himself to, the great battles of humanity, to overcome and improve its environment and the basic human condition. This sense of solidarity with others, accepting a basic humanism as the starting point for belief, is a very precious gain out of the current theological debate. Statements about God and Christ can now be seen as augmenting and developing basic human experience and not seen as running counter to them.

An appreciation of these theological ideas was made popular by the publication of John Robinson's book *Honest to God* in 1963.[3] The publication was followed by a spate of similar writing and by the appearance, in most Christian denominations, of a radical wing of ministers and laymen. They possessed a missionary desire for Christians to be seen, to be identified, with their fellow men in the situations in which they found themselves with the accent on Christian community action. This zeal was so intense that often it went too far in denying the values of the Christian community, itself to itself. There is currently a reaction to this trend and probably rightly so in the dialectic of affairs, but it is hoped that the step forward taken then will not be totally retraced since it represented in principle a necessary contemporary restatement of the Christian position.

These comments have sought to justify the claim at the beginning of the chapter that these are very challenging times for the Christian. The net result of all these factors has been to lay bare faith in a way that probably has not happened for many generations. There is indeed almost a challenge to have faith even without belief. The contemporary Christian position can be described as one of hopeful pessimism where the cry is deep from the heart, 'This only I hold, but it is enough'. Moreover, these new insights are at their strongest when we interpret them to mean actively seeking out an encounter with God in our daily lives; that we must expect to be confronted by God in each and every situation that comes along. What better comfort can there be than this message, when the present state of the church pushes us more and more into the world of experience for our search for God and the ways to serve our fellow men?

Many would retort that this contemporary view is misguided and indeed that it may be the very fact that increasing numbers think this way that has caused the decline in the church's influence and in the numbers coming to Christ. I believe that nothing could be further from the truth. Not only does this view seem to be the only one

[3] John A. H. Robinson, *Honest to God*, S.C.M. Press, 1963.

consistent with the climate of our age, but the challenge that is thrown up by contemporary life and our attempts to interpret our faith, create precisely the conditions required in which the worth of the Christian can be measured. The consequences of this development of tradition—far from weakening the grounds of belief—give a deeper sense of the relevance of the Christian message and a deeper awareness of the great truths found in the Bible which have been carried on in the tradition of the church up to today.

Modern belief and economics

Many parts of the Christian inheritance, in part traditional and in part new, are of importance to a Christian seeking to make sense of living in modern society and the rest of this chapter outlines, as reference points, so to speak, for the rest of the book, the main propositions stemming from the belief in God the Creator and in his Son Jesus Christ—the revealer of perfect human relationships between man and God and man and his fellow man—that relate to contemporary economic society.

(a) It is God's world. The first thing that needs to be said is that this world belongs to God. Christians believe that God created it, and believe that God created all of it. That means that we cannot pick and choose and say that some parts have been God-given and that others do not belong to God. It follows that our main task is to ensure that all uses made of God's world are also to his glory. This means that if a way is found if utilizing the world's resources to create greater wealth it can only be understood in terms of what God wants for us and such resources must be dedicated to his glory if they are to be acceptable. It also follows that all consequences of such human activity, even materialism, and certainly the economic system created to achieve materialistic ends, must be conceived of within the framework of God's will for man in the world. We have to believe therefore not only in the sovereignty of God over nature but also his sovereignty over the institutions that we create to work in partnership with nature and which can or cannot allow individuals to achieve their own full development. We also believe that within this understanding the concept of stewardship has to be worked out and given full meaning. We have, for example, responsibilities to preserve resources, both to ensure that they are available for our fellow men, of our own generation and of generations to come.

(b) The nature of man. Secondly, there is the question of the nature of man himself. Christians believe that man is prone to sin; this means that whatever set of systems are created, whether they are political or economic, or whatever objectives are set, man is

capable of making a good old hash of things. It may be argued that he can make a bigger hash of things under certain circumstances than others—a point which will be discussed later—but the basic proposition here is that the Christian must act on the assumption that man is more likely to get things wrong than right. But Christians also believe man is capable, with God's help, of rising above sin and living and working to the glory of God. Christians have, on the whole, an almost naïve confidence in the potential greatness of man—quite unjustified by experience. They hold to the belief that as man was created by God he is capable of achieving God's will for him. This view, however often falsified by events, is held strongly enough for the Christians to begin each time after failure to try once again to do better with an undimished belief in the prospects of success.

(c) Equality, justice and liberty. The Christian also believes in equality amongst men. It is part of the Christian faith that a consequence of God's love for man is that all men are equal in his eyes. It is therefore incumbent on us to find the means of giving substance to this statement and at the very least accepting that the burden of proof rests with those who wish to create inequalities.

This concept of equality is as relevant to economic affairs as anywhere else and its importance has always been recognized. It is to be found in the great cry of the followers of Wat Tyler in the fifteenth century:

> 'When Adam delved and Eve span
> Who was then the gentleman?'

It is there also in the great Marxist slogan: 'From each according to his ability to each according to his needs.' It is a particularly relevant issue in the great debate as to whether the present type of economic system can function to any degree effectively without an inegalitarian system of rewards. Those wishing to take man as he is and does, argue that the present system, being largely based on acquisitiveness, must let the consequences come through in terms of incentives to earn more, at least according to ability, otherwise resources will not be allocated efficiently to meet demands. Man, as a matter of fact, it is argued, does not appear to want a system that ensures equality. Even those who lose in the system still seem to want one that at least enables them to try to win rewards. Against this view is the undeniable logic of those, starting from a basic view about the sense of worth of each and every man, who plead for a system in which this basic equality is respected in economic terms as well as in other respects. This plea is partly aimed to ensure that the economic system through income distribution, for example, looks morally credible at the end of the day. But it often goes beyond to a desire that the whole economic system should be run on the basis of relationships between man and man which reflect the equal merit of all.

Along with the concept of equality goes the equally important idea of justice. This is the belief that our systems and our relationships between people should be seen to be fair and that each of us has an equal right to just treatment. Justice reflects the sense of individual freedom and is defended by our laws and institutions. The British tradition of justice in particular offers to each and every person a basic equality of respect which is the envy of much of the rest of the world. It is a respect which embraces wider ideas than simply rights in the courts; it relates to the style of life, and the sense of natural liberty and justice.

Increasingly, however, it is necessary to qualify or, at least, augment the view of natural individual liberty with a sense of social justice which in certain circumstances may be seen in opposition to the requirements of individual liberty. There is no reason why they should conflict irreconcilably since the case for both is easily acknowledged. But there is a wider concept of freedom and responsibility which individuals must both claim and respect. The view of man, of infinite worth, as an individual person yet with firm responsibilities for the care of others, is part of the Christian tradition and has considerable relevance to the task of assessing the modern interdependent and increasingly socialized life style of contemporary society.

In this sense the ideas of justice and liberty are bound up with the view of the individual. Christians believe that individuals matter as persons and that God himself is best expressed in personal terms. This view of the individual can be found throughout the teaching of the church although it was particularly accentuated by the growth of liberalism of the nineteenth century. Perhaps we have now reached the stage where the distinction needs to be made between individualism and the concept of person which carries the full implication of the social obligation for others. If this wider concept is adopted economic and political institutions will need to be judged as beneficent or not according to whether such systems encourage the full development of people as persons.

(d) The Christian as servant. Another main strand of Christian thought which has a particular bearing on the contemporary scene is the image of Christ as servant. This Old Testament based concept has grown in popularity in recent years and presents a very attractive

model for both the church at large and for the individual Christian. The view of Christian behaviour implied by the image is a personal life style and attitude particularly opposed to power-orientated concepts, such as ambition, success and leadership. It argues that these are not worthy concepts for the Christian and that on the contrary he must expect—must wish to be—more often than not at the humble end of the spectrum—of being led, of being content with lowly conditions and of being trampled upon. A consequence of this attitude is a somewhat near-fatalist pessimism often held by Christians about their likely impact on the world. It is argued that the Christian religion is in a sense failure orientated: failure not only in the sense that the world uses the term—and that it certainly expects to be—but even on the ground of its own choosing. It has to expect to be rejected. It has to live with a contemporary secular situation in which God seems to have lost or at least forsaken his people. History is full of examples of the dark night of faith and the apparent success of oppression. The Christian, it is argued, must find the joy of faith in the very evidence against it; there will be nowhere else to look.

(e) Christians care. Christians care for others. The Christian must always be sensitive of the plight of others and is under a categorical obligation to do what he can to help them. Christ's teaching in this respect is perfectly clear and the Christian regards himself as more likely to be condemned for failing to care for his neighbour than perhaps for anything else. This obligation helps to frame the Christian's attitude to economics and politics in a number of important respects. While he is required to do all he can to promote a just and equitable economic and political system in which all men are respected and given a sense of worth, he is also under equal obligation, so long as the system falls short of perfection and causes excesses of poverty and injustice, to be prepared to share—perhaps at extreme cost—with his fellows when he is more fortunately situated. For example the cry of 'Trade not Aid' which is used by the development lobby, although it may be very worthy as the main objective for development, is not enough for the Christian; he must be for trade but still be ready to give aid. Similarly in his personal relationships, the preparedness to meet need no matter at what cost and whatever merit must always be there.

(f) The Christian view of work. The church has long established teachings about the doctrine of work. The biblical basis for the view is unambiguous. Man is expected to spend most of his time with a great deal of sweat on his brow, ekeing out a living and can reckon to spend most of his working life so doing. This view of the lot of man

has been perpetuated right through to modern times, and especially by the link between Protestantism and the rise of capitalism, and is still largely endorsed by the Christian community. To a Methodist the Wesleyan dictum of 'Gain all you can, save all you can, give all you can' is an apposite illustration of the traditional philosophy. Working, of course, is not simply a question of providing food, shelter and other essentials. It is also, and increasingly so in an affluent society, the measuring rod for the sense of worth of individuals as will be argued in much more detail in a later chapter.[4] But the point being made here is simply that the Christian inheritance to date is a concept of man the worker and it is increasingly becoming clear that the Christian position will need to be substantially revised as our success in becoming wealthier offers a real choice between wealth and leisure and where the role of work solely to provide necessities has virtually disappeared. To make an understatement, the church is not theologically well prepared to advise on daily living in an essentially leisure-dominated situation.

(g) Christian hope. Although there is an element of fatalism in the Christian tradition, it is counter-balanced by a sense of optimism about the destiny of the world. Despite the many contemporary events threatening the grounds upon which the belief rests, Christians believe that all is, or will be, right in God's world and that in due time he will bring it to a final state of perfection. Christians have therefore perhaps a greater belief than average in the potential success of social engineering and the ability to turn things and people to the glory of God. They want to believe in the view that the system is orderly and under control and is capable of being made to converge on desired objectives.

An optimism of this sort does not die easily, thank God. Nevertheless, it is evident that we do not live in a world which can be easily harnessed to the glory of God. Nature itself has an uncomfortable habit of reminding us how volatile it can be, either through earthquakes, droughts or storms. The last two decades have also shown world-wide how easily established political and social institutions can come under fire and begin to break down. We have only to contemplate the possible consequences of great semi-global power confrontations either between the East and West or between the affluent and the poor to realize the knife-edge on which we stand. The same is also true within our own society. Many commentators would say that too many of the established reference points in our present society are disappearing and that it is just as likely that we will enter a period of anarchy and change, perhaps of a quite

[4] See Chapter 6.

revolutionary sort, as it is that we will remain wedded and loyal to our present institutions.

(h) Revolution or stability? There is, of course, a Christian view that revolutionary changes of this nature are not only likely but are to be desired. There is no real reason why the church should assume that the *status quo* is to be defended. Indeed there is a strong Christian tradition that takes the reverse view: that the secular arm will always and inevitably end up by being detrimental to the Christian cause and lead to the oppression of man and inhibit the coming of God's kingdom. This point of view sees the hope for the world in the revolutionary situation and welcomes change, particularly radical change. While it may be against the Christian temperament in this country to embrace this point of view, there are obviously many parts of the world where it is the right one. Many Christians and others are under oppression and are not receiving the basic rights which Christians hold dear such as justice and freedom, and the church has to decide where it stands.

(i) Other worldliness. It also has to be said that there is a strong Christian tradition in favour of the complete abandonment of the material aspects of this world; a disassociation from daily life and the set of human values that are attached to it. This other worldliness, which takes its lead from Christ himself, has shown itself in the great reflective tradition of the church and must be seen as a challenge to the Christian man prone to engage actively in the field of politics and economics. In particular he has to take careful account of the view that it may be harder for a man to find the kingdom of God in an affluent situation than in poverty. It is a point of view with biblical support which has been in the forefront of Christian tradition since the beginning of the church.

(j) The encounter with God. On one thing the teaching of the church is absolutely clear. The primary challenge of the Christian is to respond to God's demands. It is a challenge of the present here and now. It is a comprehensive challenge to be found in every situation facing him. It is an either/or challenge where the Christian is required to decide for or against God. It is not a situation in which we can strive for perfection as if we are trying to earn credit, nor is it a question of working to improve the world in some respects, though there may be other good reasons why we should do that. God's call is unconditional, and is there to be answered in each moment of life. In the decision of the moment is the choice between heaven and hell, for or against God. What God wants from us in no more and no less than complete obedience to his will in every situation. That is what religion is all about; the whole world of experience in which we

find ourselves is the ground for decision and therefore sacred. The Christian is committed to this secular world where he will be confronted by God and be given the opportunity to do his will.

To sum up, therefore, the Christian cannot avoid the world in which he is set. It provides the grounds in which he can experience God and provides the chance to practise religion. It sets the scene for man's decision for or against God and, as it is truly God's world, he must work within it to serve his fellow men. Equally in that world he must see that things are so ordered that man as a person is respected and that the application of Christian love is effective in personal and social relationships. These are the guidelines with which the Christian, so to speak, must arm himself for the task of daily living.

4 Preliminary thoughts—on the layman's daily life

The two preceding chapters have provided some preliminary thoughts on modern economics and contemporary theology prior to forming a Christian view of the modern affluent economy and our participation in it. Before we go on, however, there is one more area which needs to be discussed if the Christian's position is to be fully explored. This is the environment—usually limiting—in which the layman is required to live out his life and apply his principles. It is a constraining situation where even if the best is seen, it is not necessarily achievable; where progress in any sense is at best just perceptible; where the struggle is to achieve the better rather than the best. In contrast much Christian teaching serves to embarrass in a sense that its high ideals and message of perfection continually remind us of failure. The Christian layman therefore feels particularly under stress by being constantly required to assess his position against the faith and principles that he has embraced. Many Christians attempting the near impossible task to bear witness in such circumstances find the strain very heavy indeed and deserve a great deal of sympathy and understanding on the part of the church.

I want to discuss a number of areas in which the Christian finds himself under stress and which demonstrate, as it were, the holy tensions facing him.

The ideal and the attainable
The first comment relates to what can best be called the lie which Christians are forced to live. However weary the daily stint at work and however limiting horizons turn out to be in practice, the Christian has to believe very firmly in the possibility of achieving much better things. As a practising economist, for example, he may participate in national planning initiatives to achieve faster economic growth or as a citizen he may vote to elect the government of his choice in the belief that it is more likely to enable society to achieve its social goals. But these are miniscule movements towards the attainment of ends when compared with great promise of achievement offered by the Christian religion. Throughout the church's history there have been groups who have embraced a form of Utopianism, who have believed that the perfect is practicable

(which is as good a definition of Utopianism as any). All Christians warm to these attempts and from time to time will share the same hope. What else is that feeling each Christmas when the new born babe is revered? Christians have to be the most absurdly optimistic of men when they believe that it is within man's potential to bring in the kingdom of God. There is also a strong tradition in Christian teaching which claims that the introduction of the kingdom of God is essentially a revolutionary concept. This can be interpreted to mean in one sense the necessity for change in personal attitudes and behaviour, and in another sense the introduction of radical social changes in the more conventionally accepted political sense.

There is a logic which commends this attitude strongly to the Christian. We know the extent of human sin and need no persuading that root and branch conversion is essential if a new world of relationships is to be achieved. We also know how the absence of this conversion is reflected in the deficiencies and limitations of men and institutions which provide resistance to change as well as fail to attain ideals. What is obvious therefore to the Christian is the need for conversion of man and society in both these senses. All shades of theological opinion would stand by this position in one way or another, differing only in emphasis either in the respective importance of personal salvation or in the need for social change for a better world. The evangelical seeking to convert hearts to Christ has the ultimate logic in his reasoning which would lead to an equal and comparable transformation of society. The radical in seeking to change society takes for granted a concomitant conversion of souls whose failings are currently revealed in the behaviour of institutions.

The reasoning is heavy stuff for the Christian and when put persuasively from the pulpit still evokes the 'Halleluiah' and 'Amen' from the layman in the pew. And yet it is not really the world he recognizes. His world of experience is not one of vision and revolution. His work goes on, his relationships within the factory or office or between colleagues do not in any sense encourage radical change unless he is one of a small minority who practise rejection of contemporary society. For most people the position is the reverse. They will tend to judge the respective strength of appeal of the political parties by the degree of stability and continuity that they are offering to provide. Also in the realm of human relationships experience is seen as one of stability with few traumatic changes in life styles. The vision of Utopia and revolution, alas, is all too often kept for the Christmas season.

The task of the Christian, therefore, is somehow to come to terms with this basic duality of experience. He must share the hope of the church in better things to come and, more important, the possibility that they can be achieved. He must also share the belief in the need for revolution which so logically follows from the Christian view. But at the same time he must remain earthbound, splash around in the mud of limited horizons and limited, hesitant progress and the tendency to settle for stability and safe ground.

Ambition

A second area of concern to the Christian layman, where the church has been particularly lacking in its help to him, is in that of ambition. Society is on the whole geared to the objective of efficiency—to get things done in the best possible way—whether it be in a Department of State or in a large or small business. Most Christians have to live within this framework. The organization in which they work is an established means of getting things done and laymen participating in those activities work the system as well as they can in order to obtain the best possible results. There is a justified sense of achievement at the end of the day. In a true sense the Christian has, or should have, therefore, a legitimate sense of ambition.

The Christian has to distinguish between what may be described as corporate and personal ambition. Most 'work the system' in their everyday lives largely in impersonal terms. They are able to see themselves as representatives of particular interests either within their organization or representing it *vis-à-vis* other organizations. They help to make the system work but the conflict and compromise that they bring arises in their pursuit of corporate objectives. The impassive diplomat endlessly engaged in East–West confrontations is an example *par excellence*.

But a Christian has also to establish his own personal position. He has to match his personal actions and his personal lifestyle against the message of the Bible, the teaching of the church and his conscience. Most Christians have acute problems in the matter of personal ambition. On the one hand they are deeply conscious of Christ's injunction to practise humility, to be the servant rather than the master, to sit at the bottom rather than at the top of the table. None of these attitudes really squares with the struggle for position to become the managing director of a top company or the chairman of a nationalized industry. And yet on the other hand, personal ambition is a very powerful driving force, and often results in the smooth rationalization 'I wish to do good and the higher up I am the greater influence for good I shall be; therefore it is right for me to seek the highest job'.

Some laymen go on to do just that and sometime, somewhere, judgement will be passed on them, but most end up in the middle path of mediocrity and from that many would like to escape. Indeed, the Christian more than most, often toys with opting out of the secular game. When he is completely involved in the competitive industrial system, the grass on the other side looks very green to him. The senior officers of our churches could tell of the numerous offers of service from laymen who feel that the world of commerce and industry has yielded up all the satisfaction it can to them and they wish to fulfil their vocation in a more 'spiritual' sense for the remainder of their lives.

This point of view is suspect. There is something illogical about a man's position if he wishes to continue to live in a world in which so much of benefit and pleasure derives from the acquisitive, competitive system and yet he feels that the working of that particular system is not for him. But even more important, on a personal level, is the fact that to opt out and to find a 'quiet' life (which incredibly is often thought to lie in working for the social services) is often a flight from reality. Some people do make these changes successfully but when the business man dreams of swopping the city for a small provincial town, of quitting the boardroom in order to 'do good' in the community, the real motive often lies well below the surface. He is looking for some place where the pressures are off him, where his particular qualities are accepted without question and more importantly, where nothing that he does will create a sense of failure on his part.

It is a vain search. For failure or sense of failure is the reverse side of the coin of ambition and the thing that we most acutely desire in living our lives is to have a sense of being wanted and being considered worthy. We grossly underestimate the strength of the sociological net which makes up the satisfaction in our lives; status, performance, position, relative wealth, etc. As time goes by we steadily build up a variety of defences and props to our security which allow us to make the most of life and at the same time protect us as far as possible from the rudeness of the outside world. If these props are removed or begin to fall away the ordinary man feels very threatened. Most people achieve reasonable success during their lives in this way, but the passage of time itself can begin to threaten them. It is sad to see the years slip by and realize more and more that time will not allow us to do all the things we want to do. It is even sadder when the years also tell us that we are not equipped to fulfil the desires and ambitions of our youth.

Compromise

The third area of concern to the Christian relates to the question of compromise. Compromise is not a happy word for him. On the whole religion is about black and white, of good and evil, and all the other positive and negative absolutes. But this is not the way the world works in practice. Most decision-making and judgements on events are in the grey areas of the world and the Christian actually gets little instruction on how to cope with such situations.

There are some, of course, who, while recognizing that there are many areas where compromise is necessary, seek to identify areas where at least as far as they are concerned there is no question of compromise. This leads to a desire for a basic set of irreducible minimum truths by which they stand or fall. It is a good argument but one which is more from the heart than from the head and it may be preferable to take the somewhat more gloomy view that at some time most situations will require a compromise solution of one sort or another. Putting aside the problems of men of principle then, it is quite clear that for most Christians much of their time is spent in compromise situations where it is essential for them to have worked out as carefully as they can a theology of compromise—a subject on which very little is written.[1]

Compromise is where two sides who disagree on a position, decide that rather than continue in disagreement and do nothing, it would be better to accept a third way with some ingredients of both positions in it as a basis for action. The essence of compromise is an agreement to disagree and not the removal of all disagreement. In an ideal world the solution of disagreement would be a completely full understanding of the situation as a result of which the 'right' course becomes apparent to both sides. This latter situation, however, is rare and the need for compromise arises for a variety of reasons. One is that the situation still contains as yet irreconcilable points of view. Another is that there has not been enough time to examine the situation sufficiently fully to enable both sides to recognize the right course between them. Another is the lack of complete knowledge about the situation to which the proposed action is addressed and the respective positions of the two parties. Invariably there is often, for one reason or another, a less than complete understanding of the other party's position and associated with that point of view is often a lack of objectivity about the situation. In Herbert Butterfield's example of the rightness in a war situation, it

---

[1] Although one notable exception is Herbert Butterfield's masterpiece *Christianity and History*, G. Bell and Son Ltd 1949. See also Donald Soper, *Christian Politics*, ch. 3, Epworth 1977.

is clear that the need for patriotic fervour in order to bring a country to a state of readiness for war had necessarily to cloud the issues about the respective rights and wrongs of the two countries' positions. It is only subsequently that the real issues and the relative balance of right and wrong can be assessed.

The first conclusion to draw from this set of circumstances requiring compromise is the need for a good solid sense of humility about who is right and wrong in any particular situation. The real professionals in the field of compromise, those engaged in industrial arbitration, negotiations between countries, etc., often display a detachment and a readiness to accept the worth in all arguments and a respect for people which could well be imitated more by Christians and the church in general in its pronouncements about the rights and wrongs of society. In other words, although in one sense the nature of compromise is the abandonment of a principle and the settling of something that is far short of desirable, in practice the compromise situation of the real world often carries with it a much greater application of true Christian virtues than is credited.

Another aspect in this field of compromise which matters a great deal to the Christian is the question of his loyalty both to his institution and to his colleagues who, day in day out, participate with him in the making of compromised decisions. To take a timely example, a Christian working as a senior manager in, say, a large industrial firm may be closely involved in a decision whether or not to close a less productive plant in one part of the country in favour of the expansion of a new and more productive plant elsewhere. The consequence may be increased efficiency for the firm but at the price of throwing loyal members of the company out of work. He personally may well feel that the loss of jobs and its social and personal consequences are too high a price to pay for increased efficiency. He may passionately hold this view stemming from his Christian view of the dignity of man. To a greater or lesser extent, depending on his position in the firm he will have his chance to argue his case. But, of course, there will be other strong and opposing views and others may prefer to give the increase in efficiency the greater priority even though it has adverse social and personal consequences.

At the end of the day a choice has to be made and in the nature of the compromise situation the final result will be a package which suits no one entirely and may, for example in this case, be heavily in favour of the point of view arguing for the maximum possible increase in efficiency. Assuming that this is the case, what is our Christian supposed to do?

He can, of course, resign. There have been many cases in industry and politics of people who in fact at certain times have chosen precisely this course of action. It is an honourable course but like all good things is probably not to be indulged in too often. The reason why this is so is because anyone who takes this course is in effect washing his hands of responsibility and is in effect saying that people are making such a mess of it that he wishes to have no further part in the process. But in reality there is in fact very little joy and satisfaction in so acting. People are extremely constrained in their choice of what they can do to put a situation right and someone has to carry on making decisions however bad they turn out to be. Someone has to take today's decisions and go to bed praying that tomorrow they may make better ones.

For the majority of people therefore, for the majority of time, the right and proper thing to do is to stick with the task and to share a responsibility for yesterday's decisions, even though this course requires considerable compromise on most people's part. This applies to the Christian as much as to anyone else. So that if the firm makes a mistake by choosing the wrong policy or applies the right one inefficiently, the Christian in the firm has to stand up and be counted amongst the ranks of those others involved in that particular decision-making process. He must in that sense share in the sense of institutional sin and be ready to be attacked and condemned, if necessary, by the church and his Christian colleagues. A Christian must have his principles, he must argue them as strongly as he can; very occasionally he must disassociate himself from what others are doing but in the main he must stand alongside his colleagues and accept the corporate responsibility for decisions however misguided they turn out to be. This sense of loyalty to decisions is part and parcel of the layman's life.

The role of prophecy
This brings me on to the final point in the chapter about the limitations imposed on a layman by his self-chosen role. That is the question of prophecy. By prophecy I mean the overt declaration by the church addressing itself to society and saying 'In the name of God . . .'. This prophetic role is well exemplified by the words and actions of the prophets of the Old Testament and, if we dare to be presumptuous, has occurred many times in witness down the years, particularly in the Nonconformist tradition. The church must, from time to time, stand back and point out to humanity where it is going wrong. When it has occasion to do this it must do it competently, intelligently and without fear or favour. I shall have much more to

say about the church's role later.[2] But there is a school of thought that says that this prophetic word should in fact be contributed by the Christian laymen on the grounds that only they are in a position to understand the world in which we live and only they can make informed judgements about the rights and wrongs of a particular case. I think it follows from what I have just said that this is precisely the one thing that the layman cannot do if he is to remain loyal to the compromise situation in which he has placed himself. This perhaps is the cruellest tension of all for the layman. He may feel so strongly about the rights or wrongs of a situation, he may fervently want things to be made better, he may desperately want the church to say, in the name of God, what should happen and yet it is precisely the one thing that as a Christian in a compromise situation he cannot do without rupturing the intimate relationships between him and his colleagues in his work situation.

This is a straightforward choice for the layman. He is either in the team with his colleagues making decisions and often getting them wrong but returning to the fray the next day in the hope (never completely vain) that tomorrow's decisions will be better than today's, or he opts out, stands back from the situation and says 'I can have no part of this' and thus by act and word condemn those with whom he was associated and who remain to carry on in the compromise situation.

[2] See Chapter 10.

5   The economy around us

Our total involvement in economic activity
Chapter 2 discussed economics as a field of study, as an intellectual discipline, in order to identify these issues of particular concern to the Christian which arose out of the presumptions and methodology of the science itself. This chapter is more concerned with the practicalities of economics and describes various aspects of modern economic life which seem particularly to require the Christian's attention.

The economic system is about the production of goods and services, the use to which we put those goods and services and, in some meaning of the term, the enjoyment or satisfaction we gain from their use. To state the obvious, man is wholly involved in the whole process, is an agent in the system and is the prime beneficiary.

The system can be looked at from a number of different vantage points. It is a system which produces things. It is made up of industrial units, large and small, a stock of capital goods built up over many years and constantly being replaced and improved as the benefits of new technology are introduced. It comprises an invaluable asset in the skills of a work force built up over centuries contributing to and benefiting from the system. It contains what might be called an enabling system in the infrastructure of cities, roads and railways and many public services such as local authorities, doctors and teachers as well as a system of central government ready to promote and redirect, if necessary, the efforts of different sectors.

The system can also be seen as a set of demands for goods and services. People have wants and needs which, when identified and made effective, are the objective of the productive system.

The wants may be personal in the sense that individuals want food, clothing or cars and television sets. Other demands for goods and services are created by the system itself—the need to build new machines to replace old or investment in new equipment incorporating new technology which represent consumption foregone for the moment in order to provide more or better quality goods for consumption in the future. There are also social needs to be met such as community services, defence, education and health the demand for which is not determined by direct individual choice but socially and corporately through the political system.

The system can also be looked at as the context in which we all earn our living, where as producers, as agents in the system, we receive our reward. The range of contributions is very wide, from managing directors to shop floor employees, from university professors to library assistants. The system contains an intricate set of criteria which establishes the relative reward of people with various types of skills or, by good fortune, talents and determines rewards for various types of actions such as risk-taking.

This triangular concept of economic activity, that is, activity being regarded in terms as a set of demands for goods and services, as a system producing those goods and services or a set of rewards generated for people working in the system to produce the goods and services, is useful, since amongst other things it illustrates the way in which all economic activity is interwoven. Man the consumer cannot be separated out from man the producer.

Economics as an indicator of the quality of life

The definition of economic activity used so far has related to the production and consumption of goods and services but there is an underlying implication that the system provides satisfaction in some sense; that there is a central contribution by economic activity towards the elusive concept of the quality of life. As we will need to discuss this aspect fully it is best that a number of considerations are tackled straight away. For example, we have to be clear, when we talk about the fruits from economic activity, whether we are talking about wealth or income. Changes in wealth are linked to the rates of growth of income but at any one time we all enjoy the benefits, both at a personal and national level, of the acquired wealth of the past which will continue to give us enjoyment and satisfaction whatever the vagaries of the current economic situation and its effect on current income. In this sense it is very important to weigh carefully statements for example about the 'poverty' of a Western economy at times of crisis in the same way as it is important not to listen too much to a millionaire whose overdraft at the bank happens to have got out of hand.

It is also important to make a distinction between private and social wealth. On the whole we take the purchasing power of individuals as an indication as to whether people are well off and the amount of capital being set aside for investment in industry as an indicator of whether we are properly equipping ourselves to survive in the future world economy. The contribution to the quality of life, in the wider sense, of social investment and the social capital we have inherited is equally important. For example, Britain has been criticised severely for its poor investment performance over the last three decades. It is argued that too little of the national product has been devoted to re-equipping factories and to increasing productivity so that we are falling behind our world competitors. The corollary is often added that the reason that the reason for this is the absorption of too many resources by the public sector. Whether this is true or not, anyone who has seen how nortern cities have been regenerated over the last tow or three decades via public funds and the consequent effect on the general quality of life in these regions will not need to be reminded of the social value of such expenditures. The enjoyment of a new town centre in Preston is just as real as the pleasure from an increase in the number of television sets in use. These particular issues will be discussed in more detail later[1] but the point being made here is simply that in assessing the wealth of the nation, account has to be taken of social assets as well as private and industrial assets.

Measures of income and wealth are also of limited use as indicators of the quality of life. For example, measures of real output per head or real consumption per head cannot fully allow for a number of non-economic factors. How do we assess the joy and pleasure arising from living in the country or having easy access to green fields? What price do we put on cleaner air which not only preserves healthy lungs but allows the sun to shine through more often and more strongly? How do we estimate the satisfaction from creating more pedestrian precincts in the middle of our cities? On a more personal level the economist can only observe what individuals purchase in terms of goods and services. But these purchases are just one part of a set of activities making up individual behaviour patterns which themselves can change over time. We have, therefore, at best an imperfect indication of people's levels of enjoyment and satisfaction. For example, people now seem to be spending much more time as a family in their homes rather than in socializing activities like football matches, visits to the theatre or cinema.[2] Life seems now to be more closely bound to domestic activities such as television, do-it-yourself, home entertainment, and so on. How do we measure the implications for the quality of life of such switches in behaviour? How also do we measure the effect of changes on family relationships, especially between husband and wife, of, for example, the increasing number of labour-saving devices in houses; washing machines, dish-washers, etc?

[1] See Chapter 10.
[2] There are many interesting examples of this point throughout Young and Willmot, *The Symmetrical Family,* Routledge and Keegan Paul 1973.

Finally, it is by no means clear that all activity defined and measured as economic activity is beneficial.[3] References has already been made to examples where the act of production pollutes or mars the environment in one way or another. This debate is now well documented,[4] and there is clearly considerable strength in the criticism of those who question the value of economic growth on the grounds that the potential economic gains may be outweighed by the social and environmental costs. The motorists' exhaust fumes in the cities, the pollution of rivers by industrial effluent, the noise around airports, illustrate all too well that economic activity often exacts a heavy price from the environment. It has also to be recognized that much industrial output in strict terms is not output at all but should be regarded as an input. For example, while we may admire the intricate transport system which brings millions of workers in and out of London each day this part of the output of the transport industry can hardly be regarded as a contribution to material well-being in the sense that one would treat the production of clothes, furniture or other consumer goods. The same argument applies to many public services such as refuse collecting, street cleaning and law and order, all of which are best regarded as necessary concomitants to the economic and social framework in which we work.

The success of Western economics
Nevertheless, even given all these qualifications about the propriety of using indicators of wealth and income as measures of the quality of life there is no doubt that by any standards Britain (and for that matter the whole of the industrialized West) has enjoyed an enormous increase in living standards over the past two hundred years.[5] It has also been a process that has accelerated in the last forty years. Between 1855 and 1938, i.e. immediately prior to the Second

[3] For example, see J. Mishan, *The Cost of Economic Growth,* Penguin 1969.

[4] For example, see W. Beckerman, *In Defence of Economic Growth*, Jonathan Cape 1974.

[5] The ability to achieve economic growth in this way is best seen as a particular aspect of the scientific revolution; of man's increasing control over nature. The essence of the economic process is to blend together factors of production such as labour and machines and materials to produce the goods we need. The task of the economic system has always been to increase the efficiency of this process by producing the same amount of output with less resources or by increasing the output obtained from a given amount of factors of production. The ability to produce more now than previously depends on a number of factors: how hard we work, how skilful we are becoming, how well we manage the process and above all how much capital (machines) we have at our disposal. The feature of the past century has been a steady improvement in all these respects but particularly in the latter—the size and quality of the stock of machines with which we work.

World War, *per capita* national income (in real terms) in Britain more than trebled.[6] In the period since the Second World War *per capita* income (in real terms) has virtually doubled again.[7] If the post-war rates of growth are maintained there would be yet another doubling in *per capita* income by the end of the century.

These remarkable figures demonstrate past successes and the effectiveness of the production machine to create wealth; and there appears to be no reason why wealth should not continue to be created on the same scale. The picture is even more optimistic for other Western countries than Britain.[8] The U.S.A., Canada and Sweden have enjoyed even greater long-term rates of growth which have enabled them to reach levels of *per capita* income already substantially above other Western European levels. The U.S. *per capita* income in 1975 was virtually double that of the U.K. and that for Canada roughly 30 per cent higher. Current relative rates of growth are also different. In the early 1970s the rates of growth in output of the main Western countries were as follows[9]:

	% *per annum*
Canada	5.4
United States	3.0
Japan	9.1
France	5.3
Germany	4.3
Italy	4.5
United Kingdom	2.7

The contribution of economic growth to the quality of life has perhaps been marginally greater than the figures suggest since it has been accompanied by some reduction in the number of hours worked. The amount of benefit from growth, however, taken in the form of a reduction in hours worked, has been surprisingly small. Experience suggests, particularly in the United States, that people prefer to use any ground gained in their primary employment by way of negotiating a shorter working week to take up second (moonlighting) jobs. The same seems to be happening in Britain. Despite the post-war increase in productivity weekly hours worked have only fallen by 7.2 per cent from 1962 to 1975.[10]

[6] *The Abstract of British Historical Statistics,* ch. 13, Cambridge University Press 1962.

[7] *Economic Trends Annual Supplement,* p. 37, H.M.S.O. 1976.

[8] See Kahn and Weiner, *The Year 2000,* Table XIV, p. 161, Macmillan 1967.

[9] See Table 54, p. 133, *OECD Economic Outlook,* July 1976.

[10] Average hours worked per operative in manufacturing, *Economic Trends Annual Supplement,* p. 83, H.M.S.O. 1976.

A consumer goods society?

Although economic historians are not entirely at one in the reasons for economic growth it is generally agreed that the emergence of a mass market either at home or abroad has been a necessary condition for it to take place. The consumer market has always been an important stimulus to growth and it is likely that even when investment was at its highest the proportion of goods going into private consumption remained near to the 90 per cent mark. In 1900 private consumption was 93 per cent of the total national income,[11] and even in 1975, when a much larger proportion of current needs is met out of public expenditure, the proportion is still near to 70 per cent.[12]

The demand for consumer goods therefore represents the main stimulus to the economy and the desire for more, and the changing pattern of, demand provides the main stimulus for technological change. Consumer demand is, of course, for a variety of goods and services ranging from the essentials of food, clothing and housing at the one extreme, through the areas of semi-luxury or luxury goods such as household equipment of all kinds to the more sophisticated and growing areas of leisure services such as, for example, entertainment, transportation and meeting cultural needs at the other. The shift over a time has been in this direction. In 1900 for example the amount spent on food, drink and tobacco was 46 per cent of the total,[13] whereas by 1975 this proportion had dropped to 31 per cent.[14] The proportion spent on clothing fell from 9 per cent to 8 per cent; this decline was compensated by a much more rapid increase on expenditure on durable goods (rising from 4 to 8 per cent) and in other miscellaneous goods and services (which rose from 41 per cent to 53 per cent).

The range of consumer choice today, as all of us know from daily experience, is one of bewildering dimensions with seemingly no end to the variety of goods on offer to us and apparently no end to our ability to convince ourselves of the desirability of buying the latest innovation or improvement. The motivation behind these consumption patterns and the significance of the way we are enveloped in this web of consumer goods requires special consideration on its own and is the subject of the next chapter.

The state as an economic agent

In 1890 the proportion of national income taken by government

---

[11] *The Abstract of British Historical Statistics,* ch. XIII.
[12] *Economic Trends Annual Supplement,* H.M.S.O. 1976.
[13] *The Abstract of British Historical Statistics,* ch. XIII.
[14] *Economic Trends Annual Supplement,* p. 21, H.M.S.O. 1976.

expenditure[15] was 7 per cent. This proportion had risen to 19 per cent in 1925, 42 per cent in 1955 and currently in 1975 stands at nearly 60 per cent. The importance of, and the extent of, this increasing role of the state in our daily lives has become an issue of some considerable concern and interest. The increase is partly a result of the growing complexity of industrial organization and the need for state intervention but is more due to developments in the concepts of social need and the social provision of services. The trends have led to the state having increasing influence on the economy both as a regulator and as a consumer of output, but they also raise the dilemma—as it appears to be—of the harmonization of social and personal choice.

A view of the role and size of the public sector can never be taken in simple overall terms. There are many different functions of government. There is the provision of public services; the armed forces, the forces of law and order and public utility services such as refuse disposal, public health, etc. The case for the government carrying out these functions is self-evident though there can be debate about the amount of resources required to do the job and the quality of the service that the community wishes to have provided. There is also the provision of services which the community, through political choice, has asked the government to provide, such as the National Health Service and the education system. There are other functions, usually at local level, to provide a wide range of social and cultural facilities, such as library services, municipal stadia and transport systems and the provision of weekend entertainment in, for example, parks.

Another role of government is to regulate the economy. Although there is currently a very intense debate about the form this should take, and its extent, it would be wrong to see it as a new phenomenon. Governments have always regarded as one of their principal duties the protection and furtherance of domestic trade and industry and more recently the achievement of economic objectives such as full employment. Many of the government's activities are regulatory functions, such as the setting of standards and quality for trading, the control of monopoly, the regulation of external trade, the raising of duty on such trade and the setting of standards

---

[15] There are, of course, real debates about the appropriate size and extent of government expenditure but there are also some statistical points that make it difficult to compare government expenditure with national income. Some parts of government expenditure represents a real claim on resurces but other transactions do not strictly figure in a comparison with GNP, such as social security benefits and other transfer incomes.

for the conditions of work, minimum safety regulations, minimum wages in certain industries, etc. Although these activities may be common ground amongst the political parties government inter-vention in a wider sense, such as, for example, by nationalization, by the use of tax or other instruments to influence the location, the employment policy and/or the investment policy of industry, is much more controversial.

The government functions also now include the important role of adjusting the way in which incomes are distributed by the free working of the economy, by adopting tax policies which transfer income from one group to another to fulfil the objective of achiev-ing a more equal post-tax income distribution.

Our involvement in work

Our participation in industrial activity is intense. Hours of work have fallen considerably over the past century but, in manu-facturing, men still work an average of forty-four hours a week and there is not much evidence of a desire to reduce this figure sig-nificantly. For the foreseeable future the activity around which we will continue to plan our lives will be our attendance at our work place. To that extent, therefore, a positive view of non-work and particularly leisure will be hard to establish even though the longer term trends clearly indicate that we will soon enter a period where a view about man's total life will need to be based at least as much on a view of the non-working as the working parts of that life.

An inescapable feature of modern industrial life seems to be the existence of large organizations. Many work for industrial giants or large public bodies; few work in a small enough environment for relationships to be personalized. However necessary the size of the organization is for economic efficiency, there is a growing awareness of the damage that size has done to wider concepts of well-being.[16]

There are no doubts about some of the damaging effects of large organizations. They create the maximum possible gap between man as a producer and man as a consumer. Very few who work in a very large organization are able to retain and identity with the final product produced by the firm. For this reason, amongst others, the work situation takes on a flat monotone with too little sense of purpose built into the job. Relationships deteriorate into

[16] See E. F. Schumacher, *Small is Beautiful: A study of economics as if People Mattered*, Abacus 1974. Although written primarily with the problems of the Third World in mind, there is an increasing number of people who wish to apply a similar approach to British Industrial organization.

impersonal terms and large gaps of communication emerge between the management and shop floor.

Despite these negative elements most of us still see in the work place an important contribution to our sense of status; our sense of who we are. Most of us when asked to describe ourselves will begin by explaining what we do and where we stand in our organization. The importance of this labelling cannot be underestimated in the search for a stable personal position in society. Our job matters very much both in giving us a sense of achievement and in enabling us to relate satisfactorily to our social group. Our daily life is however still largely work centred in the sense that we see work as the means of obtaining income and therefore purchasing power. For much of what we do and achieve at the work place we expect to be rewarded financially—it is a social measure of our worth and our achievement. This is also reflected in our concern for pay relativities since they indicate our position relative to others. Also the more importance we give to our jobs as a demonstration of our sense of worth the more concerned we will be about threats to the maintenance of our position, created by unemployment, by growing old or by changing requirements for job skills.

It is essential therefore that in the view we take of the workings of the industrial organization we recognize the intricate web that it weaves around each one of us. The work place is the main area in which we seek at present to work out our lifestyle and build up relationships. It is where, as persons, we try to find satisfaction in human endeavour, where we look for approbation from our fellows and hopefully find success demonstrated in material terms as well. It is where we strive ambitiously for recognition and where we have to stand to acknowledge failure. It is where we look for merit and are judged on our achievements. It is where we learn to live and, without striking too morbid a note, where we gradually die.

Social versus personal choice
As a number of earlier remarks in this chapter have suggested, one of the most important issues of the day is the growing sense of conflict between a system in which individual choice and satisfaction is paramount and one where, either from principle or from necessity, choices have to be made socially. This feature increasingly emerges in studying expenditure patterns, where to allow a free ranging choice to each individual is becoming increasingly less feasible. It arises in the field of industrial relations where, of necessity, the relationship between employee and employer is, in the

main, socialized and institutionalized, becoming a dialogue between union and management. It is also the paramount issue in the debate about public expenditure and the role of government which is largely about social as distinct from personal choice.[17]

There is no difference in principle between, on the one hand, the situation where an individual with his weekly pay packet in his hand makes a conscious decision that he will spend so much on, say, new clothing for which he goes into a shop and buys, at the market rate, a product of the industrial system, and, on the other hand, his decision to use the public library system to the cost of providing which service he makes his contribution via his tax payments (to the government) or rates (to the local authority). It is a question of choice. The market economy makes it reasonably easy to determine what people actually want to do in the private sector. For example, in this case if our individual wants to buy more clothes, the goods are there in the shop, they are intended to be attractive and are priced at what the producer thinks is the selling price. If our individual does not go in and buy it then the producer has made a mistake and will have to learn by it by making a loss in that year or, *in extremis,* going out of business. The rule is obvious, what people want is what people go out to buy and in this sense it is a clear expression of choice.

In the case of the library service if we were able to track back and find that our individual had, during the last round of elections, put his point of view to the politicians that he wanted to have a certain amount of library services and the politicians, having been elected, then provided that service and recouped the cost from our individual by local taxes, all would be well. We would have had the same declared and revealed choice by the individual for the library service as we had for the clothing, and a similar payment for it.

In practice, of course, the setting of priorities both between private and public expenditure and within public expenditure between the various services available such as schools, roads, hospitals, libraries, etc, relies very heavily on, in this respect at any rate, a rather inefficient democratic process based on party platforms presented at times of elections which can never be more than a rough guide of what is being offered and of what people are actually voting for. If governments really knew what people wanted to be provided through public services, made clear to voters that they were going to provide those services and that it would cost a certain amount of money which had to be raised by taxes, there could be no complaint that public expenditure was 'too large' since people were

[17] J. Galbraith, *The Affluent Society,* Pelican 1958, is required reading for all those interested in this debate.

paying for what they wanted just at they do when they go into a shop.

The trouble, as we all know, is that the essential link between desires to spend and the consequences for taxation are not seen clearly either by governments or by citizens. The problem is therefore not so much a question of the rightness or wrongness of social spending but that decisions based on what people really want done socially in their name are far less easy to make and to implement efficiently than apparently is the case in the private sector of the economy. That is a problem that needs far more attention devoted to it, especially in Britain where the arguments in favour of social spending to supplement private spending are as well appreciated as anywhere else in the West.

Personal motivation in economic activity
There is one observation remaining to be made about involvement in economic activity which clearly agitates a large number of Christians, although perhaps for different and sometimes conflicting reasons. Industrial and economic activity as practised in Western economies has a sharp end to it. It appears in a number of forms and is embodied in various ways in economic theory. It concerns the profit motive, competition, efficiency, risk taking and other aspects of the economic system which bear at heart on personal initiative as it is allowed and encouraged to be expressed in the economic system. This group of concepts—if they are more than different expressions of the same thing—give rise to much heart-searching amongst Christians since, to some, a system which highlights these attributes is encouraging the baser instincts of man, or if not that, at least does not represent the best way of ordering things. There should be, it is argued, a better way of running the economy and organizing consumer activity without requiring man to act in the ways he is forced to at present and which wreaks such devastation on our personal style of life and on relationships with our fellows.

This opposition shirks the real issue. It is difficult to say whether this competitive, acquisitive instinct is an inheritance from a primaeval past which previously showed itself up in primitive survival habits, or as self-aggrandisement or the exercise of power over others; or whether it is a substitute for, or a sublimation of, man's warlike instincts (although unhappily the evidence is not very strong that we have lost the latter); or whether it is simply a manifestation of a basic heroic urge to respond to nature's challenge and take risks, like climbing the mountain simply 'because it is there'. What seems to be self-evident is that the desire to fulfil himself in a way which indulges the wish to take risks and to achieve where there is a chance of failure, to look for credit as a result of success and expect blame in failure, has been part of man's attitude to living as far back as we can go. To try to ignore, to suppress, this characteristic seems, therefore, a wholly unrealistic and undesirable aim. Instead it seems we must attempt to see this heroic drive as a positive factor and transfer the area of debate away from questions of its existence towards its harnessing for good or bad. To what purpose is it being put? is the real question that needs to be asked. Moreover, it is by no means clear that its emergence in its present form in the field of economic activity is bad or detrimental. The profit motive, the acquisitive instinct, however badly the terms have fallen into disrepute, happen to have formed the basis of the most efficient economic system so far in history. Before they are excised from the system, the obligation rests upon those opposing to explain what they propose to put in its place. There will be time later to discuss the relationship between this concept and the Christian style of life but it will suffice at this point to underline that built into our view of the way the economic system works is a view of man's natural instincts which appears to have produced an efficient economic system.

6 The compulsion to consume

The previous chapter made the point that Western economies are dominated by expenditure on consumer goods and services and that experience suggests that there is no prospect in sight of satisfying this appetite for more and more goods and for different types of goods—all this well beyond the levels needed for subsistence. This compulsion to consume must be regarded as the motive power behind technological change and the rates of economic growth achieved in modern Westen economies. We have also seen that the means by which Western economies identify and meets the demand for consumer goods is through a market and pricing system which is designed to reveal each individual's preferences and to satisfy them as effectively as possible.

The economist's explanation of consumption
This rationale of the market system is, of course, naïve and in practice all sorts of other characteristics and features are present. There is much criticism about the market system itself. For example, it is argued that often—far too often—monopolistic control over prices exercised by large companies or, more sinister, the manipulation of demand itself through advertising, or product promotion of other kinds in order to generate a market for new products, deny the supremacy of the consumer in the market place. It is also argued that the system only responds to effective demand; that the market is only influenced by those with purchasing power and thus by no means all members of society gain or benefit equally from the workings of the market system. A full assessment of the efficiency of the market system has to take into account the way in which purchasing power is distributed amongst members of society as well as identifying what people wish to do with their money once they have got it.

Nevertheless, within limits, the economist's basic propositions seem reasonable and provide a satisfactory basis on which to construct behavioural models designed to explain consumer behaviour, in the sense of being able to predict what will happen to the demand for consumer goods if changes take place in a limited number of related economic variables. The economist's prime concern in this analysis is to link together demand and supply as a means of explaining, and perhaps directing, overall economic activity. Economists would, therefore, typically, seek to explain the individual's consumption of a particular product in terms of the growth in his real income, his wealth at that moment in time and the price of the product relative to the prices of other goods. This basic model is inevitably somewhat simplistic, as the economist would be the first to admit, but its strength lies in the fact that it seeks to introduce no more assumptions than the economist believes are necessary for his purpose.

Its limitations

The economist's view of the determination of consumer demand contains a number of basic propositions. For example, he assumes, by and large, that people will buy more of a commodity if the price is lower than if it is higher. Equally, the consumer is assumed, by and large, to buy more of things if he has more income than if he has less. It is this revealed choice which interests the economist. The choice is clearly in some way or other related to satisfaction or a related concept and indeed has traditionally made use of the concept of utility which notionally is provided to the consumer by the consumption of the goods he purchases. The amount of utility received from a purchase is related to the price of the goods, since the lower the price the more utility a person can acquire with a given amount of money. Or, if the price of one good changes in relation to another, it is assumed that the consumer can find a new optimum utility position by varying his purchases of the goods which have changed prices relative to one another. But this utility is never and can never be measured in practice; it is sufficient for the economist to assume that consumers are rational beings who attempt to maximize the total utility they receive from all purchases. This part of economic theory has received a great deal of attention from economists and most would contend that there exist reasonably proven techniques for describing consumer behaviour for the purposes of explaining how the economic system works and as an aid to economic policy.[1]

Whether the economist's claim is valid depends to a large extent on the use to which the theory is being put. For most purposes of economic prediction the type of broad relationship postulated by economists seems to work satisfactorily. In taking decisions on economic policy and demand management it is necessary to have some measure of the effects of the relationship between raising and lowering taxes and, via changes in personal income, consumer expenditure; the latter, in turn, affecting overall activity and the

[1] See, for example, *Surveys of Economic Theory (Vol. III), Resource Allocation,* R. Ferber, 'Research on Household Behaviour', Macmillan 1968.

level of employment. While the quantitative effect of these changes cannot be established with a great deal of precision, the economist's explanatory system seems to work in broad aggregate and assessments of the effects of fiscal policy on overall activity have made effective use of consumption functions as their analytical tool. Judged in these terms there seems to be some substance in the economist's argument that models of this sort are sufficient for his purposes. But the limitations of the theory must be borne in mind. As we have noted earlier, the economist's view is non-judgemental. That is to say, the economist is not concerned whether certain goods are good for the consumer or whether people are happier by having certain goods than by not having them. As far as the economist is concerned the task is to find out what people want and assume for the purposes of explanation and prediction that that is what they ought to want. The theory is therefore non-subjective. It does not make value judgements about people's real state of happiness.

Also, although the economist may well be right in claiming that he has selected a sufficient set of conditions to explain consumer behaviour, many people would be quick to point out that the theory leaves a lot more to be said about consumer behaviour if a full and comprehensive view of people's attitude towards consumption is to be established. Consumption patterns, like those inheriting them, are very complex animals and people's motivations in the way in which they plan their spending are as much psychological as economic. Moreover, the reactions are certainly not yet at all obviously reducible into scientific format. And if they are not entirely psychological then they are more likely to be social or sociological in the sense that a great deal of consumer behaviour can only be explained in terms of the relationships between one household and another and against the general cultural background in which people and families are placed. The economists, many would argue, are at least pushing their luck rather hard in persevering with a very simpliste view about the attitudes of consumers.

Towards a more comprehensive view of consumer behaviour

If, therefore, we broaden the argument and consider social welfare policies, and the type of social engineering arguments used to support them, the economist's view looks increasingly limited and unhelpful. In practice much of the debate about the direction the economy should take does, in fact, revolve around arguments about social objectives and the means of achieving them. We do actually want an estimate of whether we are more or less happy under certain circumstances. We do wish to know how changes in consumer expenditure will affect private and public welfare in its very broadest terms.

If, for example, it is argued that everybody should have free access to transport we need to ask all the questions the economist asks relating to the effect on the demand for public transport of making the service free and to the subsidiary effects on demands for other goods. But we also need to ask many more questions such as whether people would actually prefer to be given that particular form of benefit rather than some other which left them to pay for transport as they had previously. The answers to these questions, although requiring the techniques of the economist, also require a much more broadly based view of social objectives and economic welfare.

In this area it is less certain that the economist is in fact offering sufficiently robust techniques of analysis of consumer behaviour to support the wider task of meeting social objectives. It is, in fact, more than likely that the more restrictive approach adopted by the economist has led to important areas being inadequately studied and that other social scientists such as psychologists and sociologists, if given more opportunity to debate the effects of economic policy more fully, would have more useful things to say.

Perhaps the most fundamental criticism, however, that has to be raised against the economic approach is that it says little if anything about the real purpose of consumption. The implication left by the economist is that man is essentially a materialistic individual who sees the goods that money can command as an end in themselves. If man is conceived essentially in these terms it is very hard to avoid a sense of condemnation of the system, particularly from a Christian point of view. If people simply consume more and more because they are for ever greedy and never satisfied with what they have got then the present generation stands very much under judgement.

So a fuller view of man and his relationship to the economy needs to be established before judgement can be finally passed. For the most part this requires an understanding of the contemporary expression of certain basic human attitudes and desires. The rest of this chapter, therefore, attempts to give this broader basis for judgement on the current affluent society.

The starting point must be again a recognition that man is totally involved in the economy both as a producer and as a consumer. By and large, whether directly or indirectly, he is linked to the system in which he spends well over half his non-sleeping time in some form of economic activity, the fruits of which labour are then used to purchase goods and services for himself and his family and a great deal of his leisure time will be spent in gaining enjoyment from these goods and services. That happens to be the particular way man's lifestyle is revealed today, although it has probably been little different in intent at any time in history. The consequence is that we must look at man's involvement in economic activity both as a producer and as a consumer as a key feature in determining the whole life-style of man. It is true that he displays many of the characteristics indicated by the economist, but there is far more at stake than that.

In the first place, it is literally through this system that he keeps himself alive. Man must still eat and drink and clothe himself in order to stay alive, and although our current affluence is such that very few in the West consider their lives under threat from shortage in respect of any of these necessities, the basic need to supply his wants for survival remains and in this sense he lives in the tradition of mankind. It is an important point to make since it is only recently that people in the West[2] have felt themselves free from the pressing necessity of surviving and, on the whole, our attitude towards work and wealth has been dictated by the precariousness of survival.[3] Although there is now a case for looking at things differently it will not be easy to break the habits of centuries.

We cannot, therefore, forget or ignore this basic desire for security and survival but it is not a sufficient or satisfactory explanation for the intricate and very affluent economic system under which most of us live. It is necessary to look further.

Another approach to understanding man in relation to his economic environment is to recall that in all societies there has always existed means by which people record and demonstrate their sense of worth to themselves and to others. This has often been done in non-economic terms such as, for example, through a political hierarchy or by prowess at sport or by other forms of ostentatious living. For better or for worse, our pervasive system of economic activity occupying so much of our time has now come to be the arena in which we offer and search for signs of our individual worth. As was pointed out earlier, if you ask a person who he is, he is almost certain to answer first in terms of how well qualified he is, which firm he works for, and what position he holds. Without asking

[2] It is not so obvious that this fear has always prevailed in all societies outside Western countries since the Industrial Revolution. There are many social anthropological studies which describe societies in which this fear appears to be lacking.

[3] Despite current affluence this thought is, of course, never far away and, particularly when unemployment rises to abnormal levels, the spectre of hunger and insecurity can come quickly back into the minds of many people.

him any questions at all you can, in any case, observe which area of a town he lives in and the style of life he is enjoying.

This is simply indicative of the human characteristic that man needs to be admired and respected by his fellows and to be praised for success; that he is more secure the more he has clear-cut reference points which indicate his relative standing in the community. Of course, no one would admit he is content with his position and there is always the logical problem of the person at the bottom of the heap, who has no one below to prop up his self-esteem, but there are few examples of societies in which this type of ranking has not been prevalent and in some societies the health of the society has depended a great deal on the acuteness with which this sense of worth is felt and demonstrated. There may, in fact, be a close relationship between the strength of the feeling of the sense of worth derived from participation in the economic process and the overall efficiency and rate of growth of economics. What is certainly true is that it would be superficial to view the productive process, i.e. man as a producer, or the consumption process, i.e. man as a consumer, in any terms which would not fully accommodate views about the importance of both sides of economic activity as an indicator of the individual's sense of worth and achievement in the eyes of his fellows.

It also has to be added that the contemporary economic process is where man reveals his inherent competitiveness. Whether or not this characteristic of man has to be accepted as a permanent feature of life, and if so, how it should be channelled, will be considered more fully later but there is no doubt that it exists at the moment and is more often than not revealed in the context of economic activity.

The task of promoting economic development was once summed up[4] as persuading young men in the Third World to replace their desires to achieve as hunters and warriors (in order to find themselves a wife), by a desire to show that they were able to earn enough to own possessions such as bicycles, clothing, transistor radios, etc. The point of the illustration is that the same basic competitive urge exists but that it can be channelled from one non-economic, non-growth orientated activity into one which is both competitive and economic, if that is so wished.

Economic activity also now provides the means by which many of the great milestones in man's natural life are expressed. There are distinctive celebratory points in the human life cycle such as maturity, marriage, peak of leadership, family responsibilities, and old age

[4] See Arthur Lewis, *The Theory of Economic Growth,* George Allen and Unwin 1955.

which are all expressed or celebrated in one way or another in materialistic terms in the sense that certain responses and commitments are expected of individuals as they pass the milestones in this life-cycle. The signs of adulthood are, for most, the achievement of a worthwhile job, the consequences of marriage and a family are the provision of a house and a reasonable level of income, the transfer of one generation to another of the leadership of family businesses is usually symbolized in materialistic terms, as is the whole paraphernalia of death and the transmission of assets from one generation to another.

There is one further way in which the interpretation of people's producing and consuming habits in relation to their style of life needs to be interpreted which extends far beyond the conventional economic understanding. This is to understand the meaning that the day-to-day use of goods and services are intended to convey. Recent work by sociologists[5] has emphasized the strength, as a driving force, of the need for individuals to relate to other groups and the complexity of the inter-group structure of society. The consumption of goods and services can be interpreted as providing symbols. That is to say, whenever we perform an act of consumption, whether we purchase a new car, provide savings for our children's education, purchase the ingredients of a dinner for a special occasion, a new set of clothes or go on holidays, these acts have to be seen as a way in which the people making the purchases are declaring what kind of people they are and the type of group they reckon they belong to or to which they wish to aspire. Some people celebrate winning on the football pool by going to the local pub on Saturday night and standing drinks all round, others celebrate good fortune by entertaining friends with pre-dinner sherry and a nicely laid table with candles, with coffee and peppermints and conversation for the rest of the evening. These are but two portraits of the countless examples that could be drawn. The point of referring to them is to illustrate the fact that the actual spending of money in each case is simply a means to a much deeper cultural meaning, the erection of signposts indicating who, in a fundamental sense, each individual reckons he is.

These activities are also a means of communication. The art of social intercourse is to be in touch with other people. The more sure you are of your position, the more you easily make contact

[5] I am greatly indebted to many long and interesting discussions with Professor Mary Douglas, whose work in this field should be studied by all interested in the subject. See, especially, her forthcoming book, with Isherwood, *The World of Goods—Towards an Anthropology of Consumption*, Penguin.

within your social group. You may even with great confidence decide to move from one group to another. The act of consumption, as well as the way in which we participate in economic activity as producers, is also to be interpreted as a way of communicating with others and other groups. It is possible to mark the activities of groups and individuals according to the means with which they facilitate social intercourse of one form or another. Besides being fundamental to an understanding of people's consumption habits, this view offers many insights necessary in social planning, since it emphasizes the importance of means of communication such as the quality of transport and the availability of telephones to the quality of life.

If we take this latter diagnosis of the role and function of consumption and link it with the other facets of our economic society such as the manifestation of the sense of worth, of competitiveness, and the milestones of life we obtain a radical view of the motivation behind consumption and perhaps economic activity generally which goes well beyond the limited analysis offered by the economist. The importance of taking such a fundamental view of the economy and the relationship of individuals to it is to ensure that when seeking to pass judgement on the economic society of the affluent West we are able to understand as fully as possibly its true significance. The questions to be asked about the affluent West are not simply whether it typifies greed or whether it defies the principle of neighbourliness by not sharing—important as these issues are—but rather what view of man in his environment it presents, in what ways is it inevitable and in what ways should it be changed or replaced? If man by his nature is competitive, is full of ambition and desiring recognition for his sense of worth, then persuading him not to be acquisitive or not to continue to grow richer is not probably the most important issue at stake. In these circumstances if we were to change the materialistic backcloth to current life, we would have to expect these basic human characteristics to manifest themselves in some other form. The view could be taken, however, that the identification of the links between the economy as we know it and these basic characteristics now presents us with an opportunity to come to terms with man and his basic characteristics and to allow, as it were, a chance to bridle them and to channel them in the direction desired by God. Thus the way may be open for a conversion of the present system into something far more worthy which would not only make it easier to meet the other criticisms of greed and lack of neighbourliness but, more fundamentally, more effectively help man to glorify God.

7 Western affluence—the case against

The last two chapters have described some of the characteristics of our affluent economy and the problems facing us. The main point being made was that it is essentially acquisitive, both in the sense that the pressures are for further economic growth to meet apparently insatiable demands and that the market and pricing system through which it operates is based on the assumption that individuals behave in a way designed to maximize personal satisfaction. It was also argued that we live in a system in which many relationships are expressed directly or indirectly in material terms. The present shape of a Western economy like ours, however, and the way it appears to be going, does not go unchallenged.[1] There are many groups both inside and outside the Christian community which in one way or another protest against it and the purpose of this chapter is to examine their case.

One justification for the Western system is that in economic terms it is, by and large, the most efficient system so far devised. It is efficient, from the economic point of view, in the sense that it provides the strongest impetus to technological change which is the motive power behind the developing patterns of consumption and production. It is efficient in its ability to generate and sustain high rates of growth of output. It is efficient in ensuring that the allocation of resources to meet demands is made in the optimum way.

Even in the eyes of its supporters, the system has many disadvantages. The system is poor at overriding major cyclical fluctuations. It concerns only effective demand. There are many imperfections preventing optimal allocation of resources and the distribution of income. The system is using up scarce resources rapidly and it can pollute.

But the opposition takes the argument much further and it is an opposition which is frequently found within the affluent societies themselves—where success has been greatest. It is in the high income countries like the U.S.A. and Sweden, and to an increasing extent in Japan, where the most fundamental questions about the nature and objectives of present Western economies are being asked. These searching questions can be grouped into two areas of concern. There are those which challenge the assumption that the Western system is necessarily the best for producing economic

[1] See, for example, J. V. Taylor, *Enough is Enough*, S.C.M. Press 1975.

growth and deciding on its uses. The second set of questions relates to the morality of any growth orientated system.

The criticisms of the Western economy

There are a variety of reasons why people come down against the present system and it must be recognized that some of them are inconsistent with each other. One argument is that there are more efficient ways of achieving growth than the present Western system. In principle the Western system provides an efficient way of allocating resources and of stimulating extra supply and demand, but it seems, curiously in the context of contemporary society, to depend so greatly on a market approach to achieve these objectives. There is currently a reaction against the individualism, and often the hysteria, of decision-making centres such as commodity and security markets and other parts of the market system especially when shortages arise. Is there no way, runs the argument, in which the need of individuals can be more efficiently recognized and met through some type of rational planning mechanism, than by having to rely on an often uncontrollable market situation? When such systems get out of control and a stampede sets in it is always the weak that suffer. Out of this point of view comes the appeal for more systematic planning in which the individual's claims can be acknowledged as much according to need as ability and whereby the country's resources can be harnessed more efficiently and explicitly to meeting these needs. This is a very compelling argument especially to the Christian who believes that life consists of loving others and being a good neighbour. He is sensitive to the appeal of a system which determines basic priorities in a way which takes care of the poor and underprivileged and the weaker members of society, even at the expense of some loss of efficiency.

Another argument raised against the present system is that it seems to imply that the fastest possible rate of growth would be desirable; not allowing us to choose, for example, between greater consumption and greater leisure. There is something disquieting, continues the argument, in being committed to a system which in a variety of ways, either explicit or implicit, creates and perpetuates an atmosphere in which people are driven to being more and more acquisitive and the production process itself reacts in more and more of a frenzy to meet these increasing demands. Many people wish to cry halt to this rush for growth and at least try to create an alternative in which conscious choices can be more effectively made between faster or slower growth.

Others would argue that the worst feature of the present system is that its working, as a matter of observation, has led to an unacceptably unequal distribution of the fruits of the system. This is alleged to be the case in the distribution of wealth and income in the United Kingdom. The question is raised whether a prerequisite to the efficient working of the system has to be a remunerative system which calls out the best in man in terms of more productive effort only by exploiting his acquisitive instincts? Why, the question is asked, is it necessary to have a system which is so overtly dependent on people's selfish motives rather than one in which service to community and respect for work done is sufficient reward?

There is also the very strong criticism that much of the growth that emerges out of the free working of the present system is of little real value and rests on very superficial judgements of the quality of life. How much sense can there be in the emergence of such bizarre demands on resources such as those of the women's fashion industry, gadgets like electric toothbrushes or some of the trivia found in many shops? Does not the assumption that this is what people wish to spend their money on grossly underestimate the dignity of man? Surely, runs the argument, a much more conscious effort to determine the direction of growth and demand is required and this is something that the free working of the market system or its marginal control by government appears unable to provide.

Finally, many people object to the life-style that is imposed on them by the present system. The social manifestations of participating in the acquisitive society are many. Most people spend the majority of their conscious day at their office or factory, much of their lives revolves around acts of consumption and other competitive consequences of the industrial society in which they are placed. There are good features of an affluent life-style, they say, but can they not be enjoyed without having to remain within the straitjacket of the less desirable social styles imposed by the present system? In other words, they are not prepared to accept that the adverse effects of the present economic system are an inevitable concomitant of adapting the most efficient way of producing and allocating resources.

The alternatives
These are serious criticisms of the present system. It is, therefore, necessary to look, at least briefly, at some of the alternatives that are offered to see whether they do give any hope of living in a better way in modern industrial society. There are perhaps two models that if considered will together give an adequate view of the alternative possibilities: the claims of Christians holding Far Left views and the

alternatives suggested by the emerging countries of the Third World.

(a) The Christian Far Left view. It would be idle in a short part of one chapter to attempt anything like a comprehensive view of the contemporary Christian Far Left view of economics. The literature on this subject is, of course, substantial.[2] An increasing number of Christians, however, are prepared to take seriously the claims of those who press for completely radical change, political as well as economic, in society. Their main criticisms are that the underlying objectives of the market economy are not only determined by those in power but are designed to ensure that those in power gain the main benefits. In other words, the present system is regarded essentially as an exploitative system in the political sense and will not be corrected until it is replaced by one in which people as a whole feel that they can participate fully and in which people as a whole gain the main benefits of the system. This point of view would want to replace virtually the whole of the price mechanism (that is, a freely determined price in a market based upon objectives of profit maximization, etc.) by an alternative out of which all the elements of exploitation have been removed and would be largely based on a social determination of needs and priorities.

Insofar as this point of view leads to a greater recognition of the merit of, and respect and care for, all people regardless of their ability to contribute and takes up the case for participatory democracy in all aspects of daily life it is clearly a very attractive philosophy for Christians. It is a highly charged area of concern, however, and is largely so not because of the attractions of the underlying theory but because of people's experience, or assumed experience, of such systems in practice. If the consequence of following this line is the possibility of political systems such as are found in Eastern Europe, then whatever the improvements achieved in economic terms they would appear to be outweighed by the loss of liberty which seems to have occurred. Moreover, many of these societies besides being repressive and short on individual liberty in many respects appear to be as exploitative as other economic systems.

These points raise highly charged political issues which lie outside the scope of this book but what does concern our theme is, that as a matter of fact, at least the European Communist countries appear to be as growth orientated as Western economies. Communist countries as they have developed so far are as capitalistic as the West in the technical sense that they are countries which, over time, have

    [2] See, for example, Peter Hebblethwaite, *The Christian-Marxist Dialogue and Beyond,* Darton, Longman and Todd 1977.

created a large capital stock with which labour can co-operate in order to produce a steady flow of consumer goods. Furthermore, as these countries have developed, the need for an increasingly sophisticated consumer market has emerged and the satisfaction of individual wants has become an increasingly important and difficult political task.

This very brief incursion into the alternative offered by the Christian Far Left is not meant to be over-critical or in any sense an exhaustive comment. It is being introduced simply to make two points. Although there would appear to be many attractive aspects of the basic approach possibly in terms of efficiency, but certainly in terms of relationships, which appeal particularly to the Christian, the advantages have to be set against the observation that where what appear to be similar systems have introduced, they seem to be associated with a drastic and unacceptable curtailment of individual freedom and liberty. Secondly, at the end of the day, the type of economic process that prevails in European Communist countries looks very similar to that in the growth orientated Western economies and therefore poses, in equal measure, the principal questions to which this book is directed.

(b) The Third World examples. There are some who look with envy at Third World economies that have yet to begin growing, or look back over time to a more idealistic non-industrial life in this country, as better models for an economic system. While some may be able to put the clock back and return to a primitive style of life it is clearly not an option for many. The West seems fated to go forward and search for new styles rather than to go back to old ones. The question can still be asked, however, whether economies around the world, which have yet to begin growing, should resist as strongly as possible the temptation to follow in our path. They have to ask themselves whether or not their present style of life with all its economic deprivations is not better than that found in the West. Putting aside the cruel fact—if ever we can—that people in these economies die much more quickly than in the West—and being dead is no choice at all—it is doubtful whether the choice is as real as it appears to be.

Such economies are ones in which the system of production is very primitive and therefore the number of demands met by the output from that productive system are small in relation to total needs. It could be argued that relative degree of importance attached to economic and non-economic elements in their social structure, is in better balance than has been achieved in the West. Also it can be argued that such economies do not necessarily look to material symbols as their indicators of state and wealth. The symbols may rather be linked to membership of the ruling class or to a priestly sect or related to the dignity of old age. All these prototypes can be found in the literature about underdeveloped countries. Many such societies, however, use material possessions as a demonstration of wealth and station. Very frequently the possession of 'luxury' goods are more sought after than basic economic necessities. Even the herds of cattle are often kept not as a sign of potential food but as a dowry for selling the daughter off to a worthy bridegroom. The less reliance placed by these societies on economic factors could be said to indicate that they are not acquisitive in the sense that the West is. The difficulty with that statement, however, is that we do not know whether they are simply not acquisitive by nature or whether they simply reflect frustrated acquisitive wants: that the communities would like to be acquisitive and growth orientated, but have not yet found the means to be so. It seems therefore that those who look to the Third World countries which have yet to begin growing as possible alternative models to Western economists, must ask whether a lack of involvement in the acquisition of material possessions is self-imposed or is unwillingly accepted by force of circumstances.

There is, however, an increasing interest in the ways in which some countries in the Third World, which are seeking economic growth, are trying to control its direction. Communist China and, even more frequently, Tanzania are quoted as examples where people have come to terms in a radical sense with the good and bad aspects of economic growth. It is difficult to sum up briefly what are the objectives of such economies but it would be fair to say that the basic characteristic is the replacement in individualism as the driving force in determining what is wanted by a more communal, social, expression of needs and priorities.

Whether such systems, however interesting and valuable they may be as examples, will in fact produce fast enough rates of growth from their economies to meet emerging social needs remains to be seen. The experience of emerging countries which start their way of life in a revolutionary atmosphere shows that for a time a revolutionary programme, starting from the abysmal state of poverty of the pre-revolutionary society, enables people working in concert to achieve a massive initial step forward in material terms. When a country has no roads then there is something uplifting and economically valuable in the community spending its weekends together building roads regardless of status and relative ability. The benefits of this stimulus may in fact last for a decade or two and in a very real sense give a massive drive forward and sense of achievement to the communities concerned. The real issue comes once this impetus has been used up and the question is not one of harnessing resources in this crude way but how, faced with a large number of conflicting needs, scarce resources are used to their maximum efficiency. Once this situation appears such countries will be quickly faced with the need to adopt one or other techniques for resource allocation which may very closely resemble those existing in the West. It is also very difficult to see how it will be possible to avoid the emergence of some element of monetary incentive to provide the sense of gain which human beings seem to require if they are to participate fully in the workings of the economic system. There are some attractive aspects about the behaviour of people and societies in earlier stages of development where they may feel that they are attempting a fresh approach to the problems of both growth and the quality of growth. It is possible, however, that it is an illusory transitional period which will be followed by one in which it will be very difficult not to adopt one of the less imaginative and much more ruthless systems either of the West or the European Communist region. This is a pessimistic conclusion reached with a silent prayer that it may be wrong; that these brave experiments will in fact reveal an alternative, viable approach to meeting people's material aspirations.

(c) The rejection of affluence. Besides the attempt to produce alternative ways of organizing economic activity which would match the efficiency of Western economies there is now building up a formidable set of moral criticisms of growth orientated systems in general. These attacks are not directed towards which choice of economic system is best in order to gain the maximum fruits from growth and its best use in the interests of the community but are a challenge as to whether any form of economic system, or whether the enjoyment of its fruits, can be an environment in which Christians can live satisfactorily.

In the first place, people point out that as a matter of observation the pursuit of material wealth allows man to indulge generously in his propensity to sin. Being greedy for material goods, going for as high a salary as possible, trying to make money as quickly as possible, all these things encourage rather than discourage our propensity to cheat, to lie, to be disloyal to our friends, not to care for our neighbours, to be proud and to get our sense of priorities out of proportion. This is a damning indictment of modern materialistic man and cannot be completely dismissed. An encounter in prison with the company directors, the lawyers, the ministers of religion as well as the petty thieves there illustrates the strength of the temptations on offer in our present society. The difficulty, however, is to imagine how the same people would behave in an entirely different society. Is it not a Christian view that man's propensity to sin would be as strong, even if differently expressed, in any social environment? Can we really convince ourselves that the modern materialistic society exposes people to personal sin more than other societies?

Another strong argument against Western affluence relates to the bad side effects which can emerge. We will discuss later the benefits of increased production and the advantages of the affluent society.[3] Against the benefits, however, can be listed an equally formidable set of disadvantages. Our society is the society of big cities with all the bad effects of connurbations, the lack of privacy, the socializing of so many activities we would prefer to remain personal; the disadvantages associated with big business, of working in an impersonal environment, working in many cases in unsocial conditions. There are the disadvantages of having to travel a long way to work, there is the threat to public health created by industrial society. Above all, there is the increasing sense of the impersonal nature of modern society; the feeling that there are so few ways in which either the means of achievement can be expressed or one's own particular identity can be established.

These are indeed severe criticisms of our present system and ones where comparison with the past would clearly indicate that our progress has not, by any means, been all gain. People fear these consequences and would plead at least for a slowing down in the present frenzy of activity so that more consideration can be given to the detrimental consequences of modern industrial life, to see whether they can at least be eased even if they cannot be wholly removed.

Some people would blame much of the disregard for the bad side effects of modern industrial activity on the style of life associated with the modern economy. This includes the relentless desire for more and more consumer goods and the way they are used to demonstrate personal pride or a sense of achievement as we have already described earlier. The thing that is lacking, the argument runs, in the present life-style is a sense of stewardship both in relation to our fellow men and to generations yet to come. If people were able to find this respect in relation to themselves, to their fellow men and to coming generations, they would discover alternative ways of living to that represented by the 'rat race' which so

[3] See Chapter 8.

many people have succumbed to and feel unable to break away from.

Finally, and perhaps the most damning argument of all, is that advocated by some that as Christians we can find no justification at all in our religion for pursuing riches. It is not difficult to find categorical advice to the contrary in the Bible and many people feel very sincerely that wealth is undoubtedly a barrier to God. There is, they say, nothing to life if it does not bring us closer to God. The Christian tradition has always had in it a viewpoint that this is best achieved by embracing the vocation of poverty and avoiding all the temptations and blandishments that go with wealth and the pursuit of riches. For this group of people the choice is uncompromising: the material benefits and blessing of riches, and even their contribution to relieving poverty and hunger throughout the world, such achievements are lesser prizes compared with the greatest prize of all, of being able to approach God and if this can best be done through poverty, or despite poverty, then so be it.

8 Taking stock

It is now time to summarize the theme of the book so far. To do this we will set the preceding three chapters against the backcloth of the introductory chapters so that we can begin to bring together a Christian view about modern living in a Western affluent economy.

Some characteristics of economic society

A number of things about our economic activity stand out quite clearly. In the first place, it is plain that we have an economic system that is capable of producing more and more. There is a basic stock of skill and technology accumulated over the centuries which is unrivalled in history and which makes it very easy to extend our command over nature, to exploit it by turning it into material goods and possessions for our delight and disposal. In other words we have now acquired the knack of economic growth. If we wish there is no reason why we should not steadily increase our wealth and levels of income for generations to come.

Secondly, we seem to have a great passion for consuming things. The human response that was obvious and necessary when faced with imminent starvation or lack of shelter has developed into a consuming desire for a whole variety of goods and services which quickly become embedded into a style of life and regarded as essential and necessary. The desire for consumption seems as great as ever at the margin. The urge seems to be the same whether it is the demand for two meals rather than one a day or whether it is for a colour television set rather than a black and white one. The desire for basic necessities is understandable. It is much more difficult to explain or to justify the apparently equally strong desire for quite extraordinary types of consumer goods. It looks, for example, as if one of the main benefits of advancing computer technology will be to provide us with boxes to be attached to our television sets for playing amusing little games on our screens. Or what does one make of the family with a 'his' and 'hers' set of motor lawnmowers?

Thirdly, there does not seem to be any apparent desire to ease off from this incredibly intense activity to produce and consume more and more. For many decades now the possibility of a much more leisured life at, by historical standards, a very high level of income has been a real option for many millions of people. There is virtually no sign of us wishing to take this option. We are clearly showing by our actions that we prefer to have additional cars, better houses, more travel, more fashion clothes rather than turn to a different style of life which would indicate some sort of satisfaction of the appetite for consumption.

Fourthly, we would do well to recognize, for example, that perhaps most people actually like it as it is. It is impossible to ignore the fact that people seem to want more and enjoy having more. They enjoy displaying their consumption habits and they get a great deal of satisfaction, not only out of their status in the system in absolute terms but especially if they are able to improve their relative position. People want to consume more, people want to earn more; they certainly wish to do as well as the next man. It does not seem to be helpful to look for explanations for this set of attitudes which argue that the system in some sense has deluded people into wanting these things or has in a way persuaded them against their will that the materialistic life is to be desired. There may be folly in it but we would not be doing justice to people by pretending that they were not self-consciously deciding that this is the life that they wish to have.

Finally, many regard the quest for affluence as in some sense a neutral activity. What they appear to mean by this is that economic growth itself is neutral and that everything depends on the end to which you put it. Or the situation itself can be regarded as neutral in the sense that, to use traditional Christian language, people are no more, but of course no less, prone to sin than they would be in other situations. Perhaps the nature of the sin confronting them is different but that is all that can be said. The poor man is permanently faced with the sin of envy and the temptation to steal, the richer man with greed, lust and other equally profound sins.

The case against affluence

(a) The problem of sharing. For a Christian the first problem about affluence is the question of sharing. Even if it is possible to justify getting rich as a legitimate end for man, it is very hard, perhaps impossible, to do so when others are relatively so poor. We can thank God for the development of conscience in our own country which has led to a very humane and potentially distributive type of society which protects the poor as best it can but it is obvious that steps in this direction on a world scale have yet to make any significant impression. Indeed the evidence so far suggests that the problem is getting worse rather than better. It is difficult to see how a Christian can set this problem aside, however much he wishes to do, in order to proceed to the task of making sense of Christian

behaviour within the context of an affluent society. The choice is made the more agonizing by the fact that so far all attempts whether in the form of aid or development to help the Third World appear to have failed.[1]

Nevertheless man, even when he is at his most acquisitive, seems to realize that he cannot live for long with the scandal of inequality. To the credit of Western communities this fact has been recognized more and more both in legislation and in the great thrust of charitable activity in many aspects of society. We need not fear that a response to a situation of glaring inequality will not be forthcoming, not only from Christians but from men generally on grounds of natural justice. It is possible therefore that, provided this response is both clear and sensitive to needs, a start could be made in justifying the affluent society in Christian terms. But it is difficult to see a way in which this can be done in the present world situation in which so many people are below the survival level in nutrition and shelter; the search for the means of rectifying this situation is an imperative for Christians.

In looking for a solution to world poverty we must bear in mind the basic point that the desire to share our wealth with others either by transferring some of it to them or by enabling them to create wealth in the way that we have managed to do assumes that what we share with others is worth having. Giving someone food when he has none or shelter where he has none is clearly desirable but we must accept the logic that efforts to enable Third World countries to grow, in the more general sense of steadily raising their standard of living, assume that we think it is desirable for Third World countries to grow to a point where they can enjoy cars, large and comfortable homes, television and all the paraphernalia of Western affluence. By and large this certainly seems to be what Third World countries want where they have had any degree of success such as in Kenya. There may be argument about the quality of growth and the desirability to direct demands in more 'desirable' channels, such as the experiments in other African countries like Tanzania, but the differences between countries that grow in that way and the current Western affluent society will be far less than the gap between the rich and the poor as of now. We cannot therefore avoid the basic issue as to whether it is desirable in Christian terms for man to create such a comfortable and rich and luxurious environment. Indeed we seem to be saying in our development efforts that we would like others to experience it as well. This in fact repeats the argument earlier that *if*, and *only if*, we are able to get away from the appalling

[1] See Chapter 9 for further discussion.

blasphemy of starvation in the world, we would still be left, but now on a world-wide scale, with the basic issue of whether an affluent society is acceptable to God or not.

(b) The bad side of affluence. It must be recognized there is a strong body of thought, with substantial historical tradition, which argues that the whole quest for affluence is wrong and contrary to the purpose of God. This body of opinion argues strongly, and in many respects convincingly, for the adoption of a simple style of life or at least for a radical change in outlook. The arguments which run through this tradition are very powerful indeed and need to be taken especially seriously by Christians in the twentieth century who, at least, are given the opportunity of an alternative choice. The modern view of the alternative life-style appears to be based on two main propositions. The first is that it is now clear, having observed the workings of the industrial system for a century or so, that the present Western style of affluence, and the productive machine that supports it, grossly violates our stewardship of nature. It does this by creating hideous cities and appalling working conditions for many millions of people. It does it by using up an excessive amount of limited resources in the world at the expense of future generations and in doing so generates an enormous amount of pollution both of the waters and the air which slowly reduces the quality of life.

Secondly, the case for a simple life-style attacks the system for being an obstacle to the attempts of man to find his God. It argues that the materialistic world in which we live suppresses spirituality, diverts man's attention away from the things that really matter in life and downgrades to a blasphemous degree God's purpose for man. This argument assumes that spirituality is the most desirable attribute and one that has to be carefully sustained. In order to achieve it we need to be freed from our obsessions about our material well-being or competitive relationships with others and from the characteristics of the materialistic society in which we currently find ourselves. Until we are free from these things we are faced with an insurmountable obstacle in our path towards God.

While this latter argument against affluence from a spiritual point of view has to be taken very seriously, the logic of the position has to be pursued far more radically than many of contemporary groups advocating new life-styles would have us believe. If we are to change, the change would have to be absolutely radical. Man is deeply involved in his present system as a producer and as a consumer, derives all his signposts of life from a system and environment which is basically materialistic. If he is going to kick it he has to kick it entirely and develop a comprehensive alternative life-style. There is no way in which we can pretend to be a weekend St Francis. It also has to be asked whether the critics of the present system have in fact thought their position through sufficiently to realize that by changing the system they would lose many of the benefits which they now take for granted such as the provision of medical services, the education system and the general background of art and culture.

The case for affluence

At this point, therefore, there is a formidable array of arguments against the Western affluent society; some related to economics, others to questions of morality. The existence of these views must at least be regarded as a warning which the rest of us must heed, but the case for rejecting our present system, root and branch, is not easily made. The modern economy provides too much of good in terms of freedom from want, of daily comforts and amenities which make possible the development of a full life that it is impossible to see it in the main as other than God-given, in the same way as we must applaud man's steadily increasing partnership with nature through the scientific revolution of the last two centuries.

In fact, we must ask the question whether we are, in our current moods, trying to knock affluence too much. A great deal is said against affluence and all its bad manifestations. Perhaps a greater attempt should be made to recognize the benefits that come from it. There is, for instance, the obvious fact that we are materially so much better off than we have been at least for centuries (that applies to the poor as well as to the rich.) Current freedom from poverty, disease, hunger and cold are vast achievements in the scale of history and can never be over-estimated. Secondly, affluence has enabled us to build up a network of state-supported services of which the Welfare State is perhaps the most obvious example. The vast superstructure of social benefits of one sort or another has only been made possible by the rates of growth in the economy over the last century or so.

But the beneficial effects do not end there. Although in earlier societies there was always a small rich minority able to sponsor and enjoy cultural activities, it was only with general economic advancement and democratization that such activities could be popularized on the present vast scale. One of the great benefits of general prosperity is the ability of the economic system to support the mass of cultural, artistic, educational and entertainment activities contributing to the full life of the majority. This enabling structure is, or should be, a great source of pride to our contemporary society.

It cannot be proved absolutely but there is also evidence that the advent of affluence has brought with it the development of a much softer and more compassionate society. It would appear to be no coincidence that the status of women has been elevated to near equality with men as the affluent society has developed. The social welfare provisions of today stand in sharp contrast to the social attitudes to people in earlier times. It is, of course, painfully clear that man has become no more peace-loving as a result of affluence and some may regret that it has given us the means to destroy on a scale unthought of in poorer times. In many, many other ways, however, wealth and the benefits of technological change in all its aspects, associated with current society, still offer hope of creating a more stable world.

Guidelines

Many of us accept that these are convincing arguments in favour of participating in, and enjoying the fruits of, the present type of Western economic system. At least it appears to be a better base than other options open to us from which to launch upon the task of Christian living at social and personal level. This is not, of course, to say that there are not great issues to be considered or that the system does not stand in need of correction. A proper understanding of that task is the theme of the remaining chapters and in order to prepare the ground it may help if certain guidelines are set out, guidelines which will, hopefully, help the modern Christian to come to terms with the affluent world around him.

(a) Living with failure. Despite all the achievements embodied in contemporary society—and we must not lose sight of the extent of these achievements—one of the symptoms of our age, and it is something of a paradox, is a disconcerting sense of failure despite all we have managed to do. It is a feeling of failure in the sense that we are acutely aware of what could have been; the gap between aspiration and intention and what materializes by way of action is plainly there for us to see.

This is no new phenomenon for a Christian. It is a result which can be predicted from the Christian view of man. Our relationships with others, our attempt at well-doing within the family and within our social or neighbourhood circles will always suffer to a greater or lesser extent from our inability to rise fully above our basic nature. Sometimes we will do better than others and with God's help even the worst shambles of an effort will be turned to good purpose. But try as we may—and this view is not necessarily impugning motives—we probably will not manage much more than a beta minus in the field of well-doing.

We have to find a way of living with this fact. If we are not careful the burden of guilt created by this sense of failure can overwhelm us and can do so to the point where we risk sinking into despair and frustration, to the point where our will to persevere and to do better next time is sapped. On the other hand the chances of failure are real and no Christian can expect to live easily with himself when he strikes the balance between debits and credits of personal living.

This view has been borne out over time in a variety of experiences; at all times in our personal relationships but also in particular historical situations such as the scandal of industrial poverty and misery created by the industrial revolution. We must, therefore, ask ourselves where the contemporary manifestation of this paradox is to be found? It would clearly seem to lie in the great issue of the divide between rich and poor countries of the world. Here is where, today, the affluent Western Christian has to acknowledge his failure to answer the cry for help—a failure resulting either from disinclination, inefficiency or irresolution. It is here that he has to come to terms with a situation which both challenges and crucifies him. Both on a personal and a social level the real insight into what religion is all about, what we mean by religious experience, comes from living through these failure prone situations with a fuller comprehension of the reality of God which can probably be fully gained in no other way. The wrong solution would be to react by eschewing all forms of action and initiative; to revert, as some have always done in the history of the church, to a passive, non-interventionist posture to the world and people around. Thanks be to God that that has not been the typical reaction of Christians. On the whole Christians have constantly returned to the battle to live better and do good.

(b) Striving for Utopia. Behind this resilience lies the strong Christian belief that a main part of God's ultimate purpose for his children is to improve things, to make life a little better for having passed by. This is true of personal relationships where the Christian is impelled to return, time and time again, to the task of creating right and loving relationships with those around him. But it has also been true in the context of the wider canvas of building a better society. I have referred to this view earlier as 'Utopianism' in order to emphasize that behind the Christian's actions lies a motivation based on a vision of a perfect society and a belief that the chances of introducing that society, with God's help, are sufficiently high to

make it worth while committing himself wholeheartedly to its achievement. To a non-Christian it appears to be a bizarre and near-lunatic ambition, which is why the term 'Utopianism' is often used as a synonym for fantasy and unrealism. But the Christian has no grounds for slighting the term in this way. His agenda for social action has to be written around this basic idea even though he knows in practice that success may well be marginal.

So here is another dilemma the Christian has to live with. He will always carry with him the burden of not creating right relationships with others, personally, socially and internationally, since if these relationships were right a new order would be brought in in which selfishness and greed would be removed. But he will also always carry with him the worldly absurd belief that things can be made perfect with God's help and in God's good time. The Christian must simply refuse to be crushed by his own failures or by the powers of the world, or to be shaken out of his belief, his optimistic belief that a better world can be built. The Christian will, therefore, wish to live responsibly and to participate in the moulding and redirecting of society even if it is by no means clear what he should actually be doing. The earlier parts of the book[2] illustrated some of the issues requiring his attention; the presuppositions underlying our economic system, the pace of growth and the distribution of its fruits, the tension between personal and social choice and the far more general issue of participatory democracy. There is no question but that the Christian should expect to be involved in these matters since he is impelled that way by his views of love and neighbourliness, justice and equality. What is less obvious is the way in which he makes his choice, how he works with others including those who choose differently in good faith and how he discerns as clearly as he can what immediate objectives are to be pursued in the interests of bringing in the kingdom of God. He must decide what means he will use to achieve his aims, whether, for example, they should be essentially revolutionary or evolutionary.

(c) A personal life-style. The real defence of the affluent society rests on whether a justification can be given to a personal life-style which is built around the helter-skelter for material possessions. The impression is that we are engaged in a wild unthinkable scramble to amuse ourselves by the use of a surfeit of material possessions derived from a growing economy. It is easy to see man as idle and unthinking, searching for nothing but superficial pleasure from the goods in his possession. The view put forward earlier[3] is that this is

[2] See Chapter 5 particularly.
[3] See Chapter 6.

essentially a superficial view, and indeed a misguided one, and that we need to search in different directions for explanations of why we want more goods and the use to which we put them. This question is basic because, if, as has been suggested earlier, the real significance of possessions is as a means of communication and not to meet basic appetites the increased accumulation of possessions does not become inevitably more trivial as the distance between poverty and affluence increases. Instead the activity has to be seen as part of the continuing struggle to achieve recognition in relation to our fellows and hopefully with our God. If this is so, then the real issue is to determine in what ways the present system needs to be regulated or redirected in order to give us the best chance of achieving mature human relationships rather than to attempt to see it in a limited and misconstrued use of material possessions as a means of meeting physical needs.

This view of the real motivation and satisfaction in economic activity applies to areas beyond the field of consumption. We are involved in the system as producers and the same human attributes and desires can be seen in our behaviour as such, as can be seen when we are regarded as consumers. We are concerned about satisfaction from earning our income, we use the system to indicate our relative worth *vis-à-vis* other members of society, as a means of deriving a sense of achievement and the satisfying of ambition. The actual day-to-day business we are engaged in and the consequences implied by it, such as our position in the hierarchy and our style of life, reveal as much about us as do our consumption patterns. More intimately, the role of the wage earner in the family is very closely linked to success or otherwise as a member of the system of production. Present attitudes to economic activity seem to subsume that man is pre-determined to be a worker in the sense the he expects most of his fulfilment to come from a daily stint of activity mainly related to providing goods and services for himself and his dependents. This has certainly been the only view that was possible until very recently but now we seem to be entering a stage where it is genuinely possible to look at alternatives and think of the full life much more in terms of non-work. The trouble with that possibility is that we are so unfamiliar with the point of view that it is difficult, both culturally and theologically, to think the implications through fully. Before offering man alternatives in the form of more leisure, we have therefore to search for a deeper understanding of man's motivation in life than we have at the moment.

Finally these comments about personal life-style raise the need to clarify some aspects of the view of the nature of man. We have seen that the economic system raises particularly sharply the need to make a distinction between the idea of man as an individual and as a person in terms of motivation and action in making economic decisions. A similar issue appears to arise in coming to terms with the increasing socialization of daily life and, particularly, in the issue of social as distinct from individual choice. The Christian, also, however, has to examine very critically alternative models for economic society, attractive as they may appear to be to see whether the view of man embraced by them is realistic. He may have to chose between a herioc and a passive view of man, the distinction being whether in an ideal state he would still expect man to display the stronger characteristics of risk taking, exploration, innovation and the ambition to succeed or whether he has a view of man in which a recognition of the sense of worth of all, regardless of ability, is given, and a ready contribution to society is made freely and passively without the display of the more fractious talents that man has displayed hitherto.

(d) The encounter with God. All these issues matter to the Christian not simply because they illustrate certain partial elements of Christian belief bearing on the conduct of economic activity—important as an understanding of their application to modern living may be—but principally because the impact of Christian scholarship, of changing religious practices and, above all, our contemporary personal experience leave us no choice but to search for an understanding of the nature and purpose of Christian living within the context of the materialistic environment. The Christian has to try to make sense of human activity, including his own, as it unfolds in economic activity. He has to define the nature of the Christian role both in relationships to others and as an active agent in changing social behaviour. He has to see those experiences in terms of a relationship with God and an attempt to let God's will for man prevail.

We have now presented the backcloth to contemporary Christian experience and action and the issues raised by it. The final task is to examine in greater depth the challenges to the Christian. We shall examine them through three different routes. The first will be via the world development issue which confronts Western Christians with the great issue of conscience of the day. The second will be via a discussion of the Christian's attitude towards, and role in, society. The third will be via the central issue of the Christian's own personal life-style and the task of making sense of Christian living in contemporary industrialized society.

9 The challenge—world development

Christians should be haunted by the spectre of the development crisis. By the crisis I mean the West's failure to solve a series of inter-related problems the sum of which creates and maintains material conditions in much of the world insufficient to maintain life and which are in sharp contrast to the conditions of the affluent West. This issue of the relationship between the West and the Third World can be seen as an extension, into a frighteningly new dimension, of the similar problem of the gap between the rich and poor within our Western society.

The issue of conscience
The fact that we cannot keep people from dying through lack of food is bad enough, to be unable to prevent the gap widening between the two sides of the world adds fuel to the fires of guilt. There is a sense of despair arising out of the failure of the techniques of development, i.e. the measures required to generate a faster growth of income and wealth in Third World countries. Western techniques do not seem to be easily exportable.

The confluence of all these issues presents to the Christian a real risk of being torn apart by his conscience, of succumbing to a sense of despair about the enormity of the task and the lack of proven means for dealing with it. However, views about world brotherhood and the dignity of man, and the deeper Christian understanding given to these concepts, leave the Christian no choice but to stick to the task of searching for solutions.

It is very difficult to deny the main issue of conscience. The period between 1700 and 1850 saw a massive creation of wealth in this country, much of which arose out of international trade of one form or another. The principles and practices of much of this activity now, in retrospect, look extremely dubious.[1] Moreover, the foundation of many family fortunes in this country derive from this trade and the subsequent benefits therefrom can now be seen in the form of splendid houses and estates around Britain. In many other ways the imperial nations of that period gained substantial material advantage out of

[1] The most painful example to recall is probably the triangular trade between England, the Coast of West Africa and the West Indies or America, in which the capture and subsequent sale of slaves on one of the three legs made the largest contribution to profits of the journeys.

transactions with the virgin countries, often by the imposition of terms of trade favouring the imperial country. There are also many who would argue that the present world economic system is just as exploitative and repressive as its predecessors.

We each have, of course, to make up our own minds on the degree of responsibility we are prepared to accept for the actions of our forefathers and how lightly we are able to dismiss the obligations they created. But there is still today's problem. The average income per head[2] in a Third World country like India is about 100 dollars per year, whereas in the United States the comparable figure is in the region of 6,000 dollars; over the next ten years, the American level is likely to increase at about 3 per cent per year whereas the Indian increase will probably be about 1 per cent per year, if that. Thus the gap, which is already horrific, will continue to grow.

Charity in the last resort

Although a permanent and sustained increase in income and wealth in Third World countries is the best solution, we are confronted with the immediate problem that many, many people are dying each day simply through lack of food and shelter. The point of the development advertisement[3] is well taken but we know we are not putting enough resources into teaching people to fish even to be able to claim we are making an inroad in the problem. But that means the Christian cannot ignore the possibility that straightforward charity itself may be the only way of alleviating the present position, however short-lived the benefits, and however uncongenial perhaps that type of assistance may appear to those being asked to receive it. For it is possible that in the present environment offers of help in that form may be turned down by the intended recipients. Nevertheless the Christian may be faced with no alternative. He must act according to his conscience and leave it to the recipient to react within the limits imposed by his sense of dignity and justice. It would be a flimsy excuse for a Western Christian to say that he allowed someone to die of starvation simply because he did not wish to offend the latter's dignity. There are times when a sense of dignity can be more important than life itself but it is very doubtful whether the millions of starving poor around the world would opt for that choice if given an alternative. There is therefore a case, in the last resort, for the exercise of old-fashioned charity even though it may be interpreted as an attempt to pay off past or present guilt and even if it makes no contribution towards the solution of the longer term problems.

[2] See the *U.N. Statistical Yearbook, 1976*, table 191.
[3] Give a man a fish, you feed him for a day; teach him to fish you feed him for life.

People are dying by the wayside, as we walk along; must we not, in Christ's name, give what help we can, in whatever form we can?

The possibility of better ways

(a) Development programmes. But there are better ways of attacking poverty. Since the Second World War a great deal of expert resources have been devoted to the study of the best way in which Western countries can build up the productive potential of Third World countries required to generate a faster rate of growth of income and wealth and thus to begin to close the gap between the two parts of the world.

The study and practice of development economies has been one of the growth areas in economics. Much has been written and many schemes proposed.[4] But success has remained extremely elusive despite the variety of policies that have been tried. It is certainly not for want of trying. Most Western countries are now committed to giving 1 per cent of their national income each year to development and there are a host of international agencies and banking institutions seeking to offer help. The magnitude of the task is best measured by remembering that we are trying to enable Third World countries to achieve an increase in levels of income in a generation or two, which is equivalent to a growth in the West of many centuries. It is debatable whether the introduction of economic solutions can move so quickly ahead of the political and cultural changes which appear to be a necessary concomitant to economic growth.

Earlier development aid was mainly in grants and loans for specific, generally large, projects in developing countries. To the embarrassment of the West many of these schemes which developing countries were persuaded to accept were, in retrospect, grandiose to the point of absurdity. There were notorious examples such as the groundnuts scheme of the late 1940s in East Africa and the massive public works projects in Ghana in the 1950s which now with the benefit of hindsight appear to have been quite ill-fitted to the needs and demands of developing countries at that stage. This large-scale approach was extremely damaging because being ill-designed it failed to generate any significant increase in productive potential and, to make matters worse, having failed to produce the results expected it led to criticisms in the West that the money had been turned by local politicians to their own advantage, thus leading to a degree of disillusionment in the West about the value of such support. While there is probably some truth in the stories of the way

[4] Still one of the best analyses of the problem is by Professor Arthur Lewis, *The Theory of Economic Growth*, George Allen and Unwin 1955.

some of the funds allocated to such projects were dissipated the disillusionment should not be allowed to detract from the fact that the idea of giving aid in this way on this scale was ill-conceived from the start.

(b) Intermediate technology. Subsequent attempts to aid developing countries appear to be more sensibly based. They now recognize the need to allow development to grow out of the local situation and do not attempt to move more quickly in terms of introducing new techniques and expertise than the local community can assimilate. The techniques of intermediate technology[5] are a good example of the much more sensitive approach to development problems which offers at least a chance of providing increases in productivity which nevertheless respect the local institutions, customs and attitudes, makes use of the acquired skills which already exist and leans heavily on what under-utilized resources there are (which in most countries take the form of surplus labour). Regrettably, however, although these techniques have now been applied for a number of years, it is still hard to discern any significant advance in the speed in which developing countries are growing. The problem appears to be as intractable as ever.

(c) The reversal of exploitation. Although most people would probably agree that there is little point in harking back to the exploitation of previous centuries in order to use them as a lever to spur on Western effort to help developing countries, there is a growing school of thought which argues that the best way to enable developing countries to catch up with the West is by, in some sense, reversing the process of earlier centuries; to tip the balance of advantage in international tradē more in the favour of developing countries. This point of view is broadly that which lies behind the efforts to create far more favourable trading conditions between Third World countries and the West. Whether this is best done by moral pressure, to make the West yield ground on the prices paid for the products of developing countries, or whether it is best done through time-honoured techniques such as the formation of cartels by producers, in order to restrict supply and force the price up, is a matter of current vigorous debate. It is certainly true, however, that where there appears to be movement in the terms of trade in favour of the Third World, such as in the case of oil prices, it has come about through the latter circumstances rather than through moral pressure.

Given the rules of the game of the present international world economy, a solution to the development problem may best be found

[5] See E. F. Schumacher, *Small is Beautiful*, Blond and Briggs 1973.

through the exercise of crude bargaining power in this form. The problem is that developing countries still have very little bargaining power and attempts to negotiate through various international bodies, such as Unctad, are meeting with little success. When, however, the Christian sees a primary producing country exploiting a particular commodity shortage or an adverse economic situation to maximize the benefit to its own people he should hesitate before condemning even if the prices of the things he buys in his own shop begin to rise as a consequence. There are indeed hopeful signs that the basic balance of the terms of trade between the West and the Third World countries will begin to shift soon in the favour of the Third World as the West's apparently insatiable appetite for raw materials goes on growing. The same price mechanism which marshals the use of scarce resources is likely also to contribute materially to a reduction in the disparity of income and wealth between the Third World and the West.

Another comment, which is often heard from Christians, is that although the gap in wealth and income between the two sides of the world is so apparent and embarrassing the gap itself may not matter that much if in fact income in absolute levels in the Third World is increasing steadily. It could well be, the argument runs, that developing countries will do better by being linked to much faster growing Western economies even at the price of a widening gap than in a situation where the gap between the two is being reduced, but where the price paid is a slower rate of growth in the West and in the Third World. This highlights the fact that the issue of poverty has two sides. It is a question of the absolute level of incomes and the level in relation to others. May God help us to deal with both, but it is probably right to rank the abolition of absolute poverty as the more important of the two objectives. The difficulty is that the types of policy required to achieve the fastest possible growth for the West (and with it the accompanying benefits to the developing countries in terms of absolute levels of income) might be incompatible with those required to reduce the gap between the two. It may not be easy therefore to pursue both objectives at the same time.

Some Christian comments
There is not much more that can be said about this world issue of development, which of course is a very complicated one, without going in detail into many issues requiring more space than is available. What I do want to do, however, in the light of preceding remarks, is make three general comments on issues which I think are particularly relevant to the Christian and have a bearing on the

Christian attitude towards development. Then I hope to bring them together to offer a Christian a sufficiently secure position from which he can judge events and base his actions in this field.

(a) The global vision. I have referred a number of times to the Christian's hold on the concept of Utopia. It is relevant when we discuss the objectives for our own society. However, the area in which it is most particularly expressed today is in the dream for a just and prosperous world society. Such a vision is well in the tradition of those in history who have managed to look beyond the prison of today's reality and yesterday's performance. The Old Testament is full of such visions; so also is our own history.[6] The Christian view of development needs to be set against this size of canvas and, no less than any earlier Christian vision, derives from the first principles of the Christian faith. The stewardship of our planet and our resources and our obligation to our neighbours leave no room for choice on the issue of development. We must share, we must not exploit, we must live in harmony. Such categorical imperatives if put into effect would revolutionize attitudes not only to the world economy but to our own economy too. There is a greater awareness of the presence of visionaries in the development movement than probably in any other contemporary movement. Much of the pain felt by the Christian arises ironically because this sense of vision is so clear.

The vision of what should be cannot be denied nor can the accompanying sense of obligation and demand for action. The question is what does the Christian do in the light of such a challenge? What indeed does he do in the light of all such challenges implied by the Gospel, which so often is so uncompromising about so many aspects of our daily existence and relationships? Jesus did not mince his words in any area of our life; whether it was to break from our families to follow him, to sell all we had to follow him, or to die for him. But this, of course, is the acute dilemma in which the Christian finds himself. He has to have the vision and its obligations clearly in his mind and yet live with the reality of the situation which appears to underline the futility of this type of hope; in fact to act in a way which blatantly falls short of these ideals.

The question is, therefore, what role, if any, this vision plays in affecting our specific actions? It is, of course, always the spur to drive us on towards its achievement. The prize is so great that no effort is too much in the attempt to reach it. This should mean that Christians last the pace better than others, are still there trying once

[6] See, for example, W. H. G. Armytage, *Heavens Below,* Routledge and Kegan Paul 1961.

again when the last attempt has failed. There is always there before us the reason why we should not grow weary in well-doing. The vision will also always remind us of our sense of failure as our efforts fall short of what is required. Without sounding too fatalistic Christians do well to remember that one of their most important, and hurtful, tasks in life generally, but particularly in the field of social action, is to find a way of living with, of being reconciled to, failure. The blessed punishment of the sense of failure against which we have to live our lives is always with us and nowhere is that more apparent than in this issue of world poverty. These remarks are not intended to encourage the Christian to try any the less hard or to lapse into despair—far from it—but simply to make the point that the essence of Christian living and action is the reaction to the admixture of the enabling power of vision and the reality of performance in practice.

(b) The nub of the development problem. It would be comforting if, from this statement of the over-riding obligation of the Christian to try and tackle the development problem, we could turn to the technicians and the theoreticians for a speedy resolution of the problem. It would be helpful if the problem could be reduced to the question of speed at which a solution is achieved. Unfortunately the experience of the past decades suggests that the problem is much more deeply rooted than that; it is not difficult indeed to become intensely pessimistic about the chances of finding solutions at all to this complex problem.

There are many alternative proposals for increasing the chances of more rapid growth in developing countries. Some have already been mentioned such as the application of intermediate technology. Obviously the social infrastructure of a country is also crucial. Countries need roads, an efficient system of government, a basic educational system, all of which if absent to any degree can seriously impede progress towards a wealthier society. Productive investment is also essential in many areas of economic activity. Output per head in most cases will only be increased if there are machines to work with and machines have to be bought out of savings or out of money lent or given from outside the country. On the whole the more investment and capital there is in a country, the greater its potential for rapid growth. A suitable international environment is also necessary. Money needs to be borrowed from abroad and therefore the conditions under which it is borrowed must not be too inhibiting in terms of rates of repayment or in dictating the ways in which the money has to be used. Anything that can be done to improve the relative exchange rate and the terms of trade for the commodities produced by the Third World countries is clearly also desirable and the greater the success in this area again the greater the chance of success for a growth policy within these countries. Outside technicians and consultants are also necessary perhaps for a long period of time to make up for the basic lack of skills amongst people of the country.

And yet when all these things have been done, and in most countries a great deal of this sort of activity has taken place since the war, there remains a feeling that an essential ingredient is still missing. In one sense it can be called motivation, but probably it is best described as a basic lack of experience in working in an advanced industrialized type of economy. An enormous amount of training has gone into producing managers, consultants, accountants, engineers and the like and this must be to the good. There are limitations, however, to the value of such training. We now have to recognize that the equivalent product in the West—for example, the junior line manager in a medium sized company—is not simply a product of an educational system and subsequent training on the factory floor. There are basic skills and attitudes towards the Western style of industrial life which we literally begin to attain in our nurseries. The toys we played with as young children, the games we played and the whole environment in which, within the family, we were trained and disciplined to think about daily affairs carries with it an underlying, conceptual approach to industrial life which is then eagerly utilized in adult life as people take up their respective professions. The little boy tinkering with the mechanics of his tank or his bicycle is beginning the education which will eventually make him a first-class production engineer. The children playing Monopoly around the Christmas fire are perhaps the financial directors of the future! How can the performance of people brought up in this environment be compared with a member of a developing country, however intelligent he is, who has been raised in a village culture and economy, in which his only contact with Western ideas (essential to participating in a Western industrial style economy) is gleaned from a school education followed by advanced training for two or three years? There is no way in which the latter can absorb the basics of the system to the extent that he can reproduce the performance of the indigenous Western entrepreneur. One of the tragedies is that the importance of this essential ingredient is not apparent and not sufficiently recognized. It is lost sight of in the mass of qualifications and intensive training heaped upon the elite group of potential leaders in developing countries. This factor argues very strongly for the continuance of intensive support in terms of personnel by the West which unhappily is not so easily accepted by those holding legitimate nationalist views and wishing to retain the dignity of operating free of outside support.

One consequence of this situation for the Christian, however, is that he must consider very seriously whether he is able to offer, at least for a limited period, his own skills and services. A visit to a Third World country will quickly confirm the vast traffic in devoted service by people, mostly young people from the West; service freely given and freely accepted. The need is still great and requires a response from all ages and all walks of life. The contribution that could be made by British managers or professional men on retirement has hardly yet been tapped. Of course, such offers have to be made in humility and with great care so as not to offend the natural dignity of the citizens of the country concerned but there is plenty of evidence to show that a great contribution of mutual advantage can be made by those who sincerely offer.

(c) The lesson of history. There is an uncomfortable aspect to the development issue, yet to be touched on. The purpose of economic theory is to rationalize and explain behaviour over the past. By and large current economic theory is able to pinpoint cause and effect in the economic system, to explain behaviour moderately well, and thereby indicate, if things require to be changed to achieve different objectives, what course of action is necessary. There is a temptation out of all this to regard the task of development, i.e. the raising of the potential of Third World countries to increase their wealth and income, as something to which the answer can be found in, as it were, a glossy-backed manual on economic development. This manual would explain what reasonable men have to do in a reasonable manner in order to enable their country to move from one rate of growth to another. The manual would embody the distilled wisdom of Western economic experience and carry with it the support of the big international financial institutions provided the recommended actions were taken. Out of this basic philosophy would come the construction of development plans with the aid of outside experts, the attempts to exploit different markets within the framework of international regulations such as those set down by the International Monetary Fund and the General Agreement on Trade and Tariffs. The whole operation would look smooth and glossy and very reasonable and logical.

And yet in one sense history has not been like that. Scholars still disagree on the causes of economic growth in Western countries. For example there is still much dispute about the nature and origins of the British industrial revolution. Where one can discern signs and causes, however, they do not seem to fit into the smooth, reasonable explanation of the economists and economic historians. If one had to hazard a guess at the largest single ingredient in the stimulation of economic growth it would appear to be one form or another of exploitation. The British industrial revolution probably owed as much to the exploitation of overseas markets as to anything else. Perhaps the largest single factor affecting the growth in the United States was the ability to exploit virgin lands inland from the coast. The earlier wealth of the Spanish Empire most certainly owes a great deal to the exploitation of precious metals in Central America and there are many other examples where, either fortuitously or not, the governing classes of a country were able to generate high levels of income which in turn led to further wealth creation.

The question is whether the rational attempts to grow which are imposed on Third World countries by the Western dominated economic and financial system will ever be able to match the drive and consequences of the old style exploitative stimuli? It is interesting, but perhaps somewhat alarming, to note that in a number of countries in the Third World which seem to be performing better than others, the possible reason seems to be the emergence of small elitist groups dominating the growth of the economy and determinedly sitting on the sources of wealth creation. However uncomfortable it is to recognize these activities and however much they run against, not only the economic presuppositions which others are seeking to impose on the country concerned, but also moral standards as well, one cannot avoid the conclusion that perhaps these very activities contain the seeds of growth for those countries which in a similar fashion enabled Western countries to grow in their own respective points of history. In its fundamentals the whole Western style of economic activity is both exploitative and acquisitive and unless we wish to change the system entirely and replace it by either an equally efficient alternative system or abandon the game of acquisition, we may have to recognize that the only way for Third World countries to join the Western ranks may be to give a much fuller rein to exploitation than the present rules of the club seem to allow.

What needs to be said to the Christian who takes these questions seriously? In the first place he must surely hold on to his ideals of a world brotherhood and a world economy in which human rights and the needs of our fellows are respected to the utmost of our ability. If we lose that dream we are lost for ever. And yet having said that the Christian must recognize the reality of the world in which he lives. He must recognize that he exists within human institutions which reflect all too human aspirations and are prone to all too human errors and failures. He must therefore live with the divine tension between the ideal and the practicable as he has always had to.

However, he has in the world context to seek to give real meaning to concepts of neighbourliness and love and this must mean in the first instance, being ready, for whatever motivation and for whatever reason, to be in essence charitable and to meet the cry of anguish of his brother from whatever part of the world the cry is heard. There is, in other words, a basic need for the Christian to respond plainly and simply by giving money and resources in response to need without creating obligations. He must, however, still retain hope that there are more efficient and sustained ways of reducing poverty and gross inequalities between countries. He must therefore support, perhaps in a way and to a degree as yet unattained, all efforts to generate Western style economic activity within the Third World, and must recognize the essential part that has to be played by dedicated men working abroad in Third World countries. Here indeed is the twentieth-century missionary challenge!

10   The challenge—social planning

If the world development issue is a constant reminder of the task
ahead the fruits of progress more immediately around us illustrate
our potential to do good and to build a just and humane society.
More than an industrial revolution took place two hundred years
ago. It triggered off a sequence of events, yet to be finished, which
have affected all aspects of society, economic, political and social
and cultural. An element in the process permitting change has
been the increased command over resources which has allowed so
many social objectives to be implemented; the abolition of poverty, the provision of better housing, schools, hospitals and roads
and the support of a network of social services. The same increasing command over resources has also provided the phenomenal
rise in our personal standard of living. One result of all these
changes is that we now live in a very complex industrial society
where the means of control, in the technical sense, are very complicated, not easy to identify and often work inadequately. This
statement is true of relationships within industry, of modern me-
tropolitan life and of the political process itself. It is not surprising
therefore that in all these three areas there are growing pressures
to examine the basis on which the present institutions operate (and
methods of controlling them) to see whether changes are necessary.

The obligation of the Christian
Christians must join in this task of critical examination. They must
do this by offering a Christian understanding of the nature of society
and the values underlying it and by offering objectives towards
which society should move. The Christian should also be ready to
propose the ways and means by which society should step by step
move in the appropriate direction—lest he be accused of being
impractical, the deadliest of secular sins! The Christian is also
required to bring to this task an underlying optimism that man is
capable of improving his lot and changing society for the better. It is
not a belief that is shared by all men at all times and Christians,
basing their view on the nature of man and an assessment of historical experience, appreciate the high risk of failure that we run,
personally and in society, of getting things wrong. Nevertheless the
Christian must build on hope, however much events seem at the

time to contradict him. This message of hope in religion requires us to have visions and to dream dreams.

This visionary hope has as often as not expressed itself in grand designs for the improvement of society. The great aspirations, as much from the heart as the head, for a society in which men live in peace, where there is freedom from want and the full life is made possible, have been present in most generations. Indeed our history is riddled with practical experiments attempting to implement this new world; the Utopian movements in evidence in almost every century, the constitutional revolution of the Commonwealth period and the experiments of Robert Owen and his followers in the beginning of the nineteenth century come to mind as examples. They have all so far failed in the sense that they have left behind little of practical value but they still remain as signs of what could have been; what man, under God, is capable of envisaging. Despite their failure, they act as an encouragement to future generations to believe a little more in the possibility of achieving perfection. Aspirations of this sort are never far away from our hearts even today. We can see modern glimpses, from time to time, in, for example, the words of the preamble to the Beveridge Report, in the sermons of Martin Luther King, in the speeches of President Kennedy. The Christian can, with pride, and must in duty, carry these visions of what is possible, by the grace of God, with him all the time. They are the rumours of hope that urge us on to better things.

And yet the Christian above all has to be a realist. Against the indomitable hope of man has to be set the reality of failure. As a matter of experience humanity has not done that well. For every social improvement each generation can regrettably produce crimes against God and man to match. Even when goodwill is there, ignorance or faint heart permits little success. Progress in practice towards these great objectives is often minimal and a far cry from what we would like; so far away in fact that often it does not seem apparent that the slow meander along the path is leading anywhere. As has already been said there is a divinely imposed tension between idealism and practicality with which all Christians must live. We are, for example, very far away from creating a just society and one in which rewards are distributed equitably. We are, in general, preoccupied with materialistic things to the point where we are in danger of losing sight of God. There is much violence and hate in our society. And yet the present offers so many ways in which the same social resources could be used to achieve a style of society of a quality without equal in history and with a capability to meet need and achieve general well-being. That is perhaps the more basic of the dilemmas facing us; once we have had sight of heavenly peaks, it is hard, very hard, to stay in the valley.

The form which our contemporary society takes determines, in many respects, the ways in which we as persons are presented with moral decisions. In our industrial society men spend a great deal of their time engaged in business activity. If there is to be business activity, therefore, we must find ways of distinguishing between good and bad businessmen so that we can judge whether people are conforming to standards of moral behaviour. More generally, the consumer goods society poses a whole variety of moral issues largely related to materialism, such as greed and envy, which we have to tackle in our attempt to live according to our principles in relation to our fellow men and God. Besides being, therefore, an object of Christian concern in its own right present-day society has to be seen as the environment in which moral choice is made.

Should the Christian bother at all about the direction in which modern economic society is moving? Should the Christian be involved at all in social change? It would be a fatal mistake to fall into the error of assuming that such activity was the be all and end all of Christian living. We do not gain access to God by making the world a better place, nor is he likely to be much comforted by our professions of good works or good intent. The crucial encounter with God, the one that really matters, is couched entirely in terms of obedience; are we, when we come face to face with God, prepared to be obedient or not? This confrontation as such has nothing to do, in the first instance, with the state of the world, the well-being of humanity or our particular moral performance as individuals. In that sense religion is not about social engineering or human and social progress. However, having said that, we must go on to recognize that the logical consequence of our obedience to God is the acceptance of many, important, even if subsidiary and secondary, implications of obedience under God. We *are* to love our neighbours. We *are* to care for the poor and needy. We *are* to live the full life under God. We *are* to respect God's world. These are the ways in which the consequences of obedience to God have to be worked out. They are no less decisive and crucial for being derivative rather than the central issue in our encounter with God.

Some contemporary issues
The Christian attitude towards society must therefore be a positive one committed to change and to the removal of things which impede progress towards social goals. Our present generation has more than its fair share of social, economic and political questions many

of which lie outside the scope of this book. But people are particularly concerned about what optimum rate of economic growth, if any, to go for and what will be the best means, technical and institutional, of achieving it. There is great interest in the proper role and value of public sector activities and the priority to be given to them. There is an anxious search for an adequate critique by which to judge the efficacy of public sector policies. There are also many questions being raised about the feasibility of achieving many commonly accepted social objectives. Underlying most, if not all, of these major issues is a concern to give meaning to personal aims and ambitions in the context of a society in which there is increasing need to recognize social as distinct from individual interests.

Since the end of the Second World War Britain has engaged vigorously, probably more than for a long time past, in discussions about social and economic objectives. There have been the ongoing debates about economic growth and planning, about the role of parliamentary democracy in relation to other power groups, about devolution and, above all, about our role in the world as the withdrawal from Empire has been completed and we have linked more formally with Continental Europe. Within society the pace of change of social conventions has also been extraordinarily fast and has affected all aspects of social and personal life, many of which have had a bearing on attitudes in the industrial field. There are mounting pressures for more industrial democracy and for more participation in local politics. It is indeed hard to imagine a thirty-year period in which there has been greater social change or debate about means and objectives except in periods of great national crises such as war.

(a) The need for debate. The first point that has to be made therefore is the rather trite one of saying that the need for the fullest possible debate about objectives is vital. When the sense of direction becomes blurred, when society is stumbling and fumbling from one situation to another, there is a great charge on people with a sense of responsibility to help identify and choose between alternative courses. The general theme of this book presents a very good example of this need. At the moment it appears to be an unresolved question whether or not we in Britain wish to devote most of our energies to achieving the maximum possible rate of economic growth, in order to enjoy the increase in material benefits that would result, or whether we now wish to ease up by simply maintaining standards at about the present levels. It is essential that the alternatives implied by this choice are clearly spelt out. It is a matter of great debate and, in one sense, a society can be judged by the way

in which it facilitates such a debate, whether it can carry the debate on without too much damage to its social structure. Many indeed argue against provoking such debate in other countries on the grounds that it would be too disruptive to the existing social framework. One of the valid claims for the British society, however, appears to be the stability of its social institutions and its ability to debate such things without fear of grave damage to that social structure.

(b) The basis of debate. It goes without saying in this country that such debates should be conducted democratically. As the birthplace of democracy, within the context of a modern industrial society, we have well tried and efficient institutions enabling the democratic process to proceed smoothly and satisfactorily and, on the whole, openly. It would be wrong, however, noí to recognize that in a number of respects British society, in comparison with other countries, is not sufficiently open, to an extent that inhibits the democratic process. Many of our institutions appear to have a natural tendency to operate in secret. Secrecy ensures a monopoly of information and that monopoly enables institutions to retain, to a large degree, the initiative in the timing and method of presenting their case. Outsiders are thereby disadvantaged and a balanced public view is inhibited.

Of course, there are arguments that can be called in aid for such secrecy, some of which have to be listened to seriously, such as the risk to commercial or national interests and security, but our present system seems too often to place the burden of proof for the release of information on those wanting it, whereas the onus should be the other way around. Moves of successive governments in the direction of releasing more information, especially recent legislation requiring similar action by companies and other bodies, are very much to be welcomed. The concept of community politics and decision-making will only be realized when there is confidence that the information system created to assist such activities is genuinely designed to serve society rather than any particular group.

Open and public participation and the provision of information to all as a basis for participation is a desirable thing and very much to be welcomed by those who believe in the value of community decision-making processes. It must not be forgotten, however, that the privileges bestowed by such a policy carry with them an equal responsibility. The consequence, for example, of trade unions or shareholders receiving the fullest possible information about the activities of the companies in which they work (or own), while a great gain in one sense, means that trade unionists and shareholders are thereby committed to and responsible for, in association with management of those companies, the very life and survival of those companies. To ask to participate, to be given the means to participate in the affairs of an institution, carries with it a commitment to that institution's problems and their solution. However much one seeks to change objectives, and the means of achieving them, in the light of freer information, at the end of the day, participation means the acceptance of responsibility. The same is true at national level. Of course it is desirable and commendable to set up an information system and a democratic process that enables people to participate but the object of the exercise is to take decisions, many of which may be unwelcome, in order to set society on the path to achieving its objectives. A proper democratic process and an adequate supply of information leaves citizens no choice but to commit themselves wholeheartedly to the decision-making process and to take their share of the responsibility of carrying out the required action.

The Christian must, therefore, support those who press for an adequate means of working for a better society; which will involve the best framework for identifying objectives, a proper process in which people can participate, an information system which is open and sufficient for the purpose, and not the monopoly of any one particular group, and above all, a sense of responsibility and commitment to courses of action which emerge out of the more open situation.

(c) The case for economic growth. On a very broad canvass, e.g. that of world economic development during the coming century, the claims of the ecologists that we are consuming resources far too rapidly have some point. There is no doubt that with present technologies and present rates of consumption the world will soon exhaust known resources of many raw materials or, at least, not provide enough for the world generally to achieve the standards of living at present enjoyed by the West. The economist may, with a certain amount of justification, argue that experience so far has shown that society is immensely adaptive in turning from one supply to another and that somehow fresh sources of energy and materials will be found to replace those that are currently wasting. But even if one is inclined to favour the economists' argument against that of the ecologists the consequences of the economists being wrong are so frightening that the gloomier viewpoint has to be taken as the working assumption and an increased concern for the care of our planet at large encouraged.

It is difficult, however, on the other hand, not to accept that in the more immediate timescale, and looking more parochially at the

United Kingdom economy on its own, plans should be built around an objective of a steady rate of economic growth for the next decade or so. There is no doubt that the majority of people look forward to a sustained period of full employment and reasonable growth in real incomes, in contrast to the turbulence and constraints of the past decade. Expectations are therefore strong for a steady improvement in the standard of living even if the rates of growth of our competitors cannot yet be emulated. The benefits of this growth in real income will be exploited largely in the area of private spending but the need is also becoming increasingly recognized for additional resources to improve and extend public services. The respective priority between these two demands, private and public spending, will be discussed later but neither can be achieved without growth and it would, I think, be an unacceptable shock to most to decide at this time deliberately to slow down or stop efforts to improve the rate of economic growth in Britain.

(d) The means of achieving economic growth. The fruits of growth can be used in many ways and much of what I say later bears upon the right approach to the use of resources, but there is still debate in this country about the best system to adopt for producing growth. The one we have is essentially a mixed system involving large private and public sectors (including nationalized means of production). There are at present groups in our society wishing to move away from this middle position either in the direction of a more thoroughly private enterprise system or, in the other direction, of a more comprehensive publicly controlled system. The likelihood of Britain moving to either of the two extremes seems relatively small. Our past history reveals a pragmatic inclination to favour middle courses and the experiences of Western countries generally seems to have led to a convergence on to the mixed type of system. Nevertheless, it must be remembered that alternative models to our present one exist and are vigorously advocated by some. Perhaps in the current climate of social uncertainty the choices of making a radical departure from the past have heightened.

Even if, however, we remain with a mixed system the case for some type of planning framework (avoiding the ideological interpretation of the word planning) seems strong. Simply on the lowest level of providing information between partners in the growth process it seems essential that government, management and unions should discuss jointly objectives for the next few years and the ways to achieve them so that each can encourage the other to mutual benefit. As a minimum this would argue for the strengthening of the machinery already in existence in the form of the

National Economic Development Council, but it could be argued in view of our poor growth performance over the last two or three decades that much more needs to be done—perhaps even in the scale of French planning procedures.

One consequence of this increased planning activity would hopefully be a realistic view of present industrial attitudes, the possibilities of change and the consequences of not changing. Many attempts have been made since the war to diagnose the cause and prescribe a cure for Britain's relatively poor economic performance and recent administrations, both Labour and Conservative, have rightly increased their concentration in this field. But it still remains a fact that as a nation we are growth orientated as consumers—that is, we have aspirations that can only be met by a much faster rate of economic growth—but appear not to be growth orientated as producers—that is, we have an industrial system, whether it be due to old equipment, poor management, union attitudes, the general fiscal climate, the loss of empire or something else, which does not produce, and perhaps does not want to produce, goods in the way our competitors do. A decision that economic growth should remain our objective must carry with it a set of consequential decisions affecting the productive process which will enable that faster rate of growth to be achieved.

(e) The quality of growth. Private consumption represents about 70 per cent of national income and is the largest single use of resources. What we spend our money on as consumers is, of course, enormously varied and covers a spectrum of needs ranging from the absolutely essential to the most frivolous. Many of us would wish for an improvement in quality in private spending to reduce the risk of our society being condemned as wasteful, unthinking and superficial. But the theme of Chapter 6 was that the motivation behind consumption is a subtle and deep one. If there is to be a different attitude to spending and a change in consumption patterns, the change is required on a personal and spiritual plane. Certainly attempts to block tendencies towards 'undesirable' spending without assessing the underlying pressures in these directions will be doomed to failure except at the margin.

(f) The role and size of the public sector. The exact role and extent of public sector activity is a matter of great debate. The extreme points of view are expressed in the view of those who argue, on doctrinaire grounds, for an increased, perhaps complete, extension of public control over all economic activity at the one extreme to those with equally doctrinaire views who want minimal or zero interference by the public sector, implying the smallest possible tax

burden (raising no more money than is required to pay for basic essential government services). These are extreme views, but there are more respectable ones away from the extremes which still conflict. One group of ideas which can be broadly represented by the writings of Professor Galbraith[1] argues that a large public sector is now with us to stay and must be seen as a necessary and valuable contribution to the quality of life. This school of opinion argues that for a variety of reasons, mainly stemming from views on the functioning of the private enterprise system, far too little attention, and resources, is given to the provision of public services in comparison to private sector facilities. The result is a public sector poorly supported and lacking in quality.

The opposing view, however, which has to be taken equally seriously, rests on a set of fears about the consequences of the growth of the public sector: the fear that a democratic system allows and encourages politicians to indulge in public sector projects which because they have to be paid for one way or another by taxes stifles growth in the private sector, reduces incentives to work and will ultimately kill the goose that lays the golden private sector egg on which public sector projects must ultimately rely for finance.

It seems reasonable in seeking for a judgement on these two views to search for a position which contains the best of both arguments. It must surely be admitted that the public sector has a large part to play in providing services which contribute at least as much to the quality of life as anything produced in the private sector. This being so it is desirable to have these services provided at the highest possible quality and to recognize fully their contribution to the quality of life. On the other hand we can have no more public sector services than we can afford. The word 'afford' in this context represents a choice i.e. between paying taxes for public services and spending the money on goods produced by the private sector through the market place. How this choice is actually made is ill-defined since it is only made clear (and poorly at that) through the operation of the democratic process. There is clearly, however, a limit at any one time to the size of public sector people prepared to support and equally clearly politicians have a tendency to ignore that limit and try to go beyond it. There is, therefore, a common sense and efficiency argument which says we should do what we want to by way of providing public services but that we should be equally sure we know what we are doing and that we are able, and willing, to accept the taxation implications.

[1] *The Affluent Society,* Pelican 1958.

(g) Impediments to achieving social goals. The massive increase in purchasing power of the majority of people raises another issue relating to choice and to social objectives. The dilemma has been forcibly put by Fred Hirsch[2] who argued that it is possible that many of the social and economic objectives presently being set by society are inherently unobtainable. The point is that, in so far as the aims of the majority are to imitate the living patterns of the minority, they will fail because much of the advantage of the minority position rests on the fact that it is a minority position. An example is the increase in leisure activities such as weekends in the country and the possession of second homes. The attraction of these pursuits rests very much on the fact that only a few are doing the same thing. Once everybody tries, the congestion on the roads, the number of people searching for out-of-the-way places will destroy the very amenity being sought. The same phenomenon is also evident in other areas of activity such as conspicuous consumption where the enjoyment, if that is the right word, hitherto has been found in the fact that only a minority were able to indulge in it. A mass-produced version of the latest Paris fashion can now be made available in the High Street so rapidly and so cheaply that the exclusiveness of owning the real thing virtually disappears. The same is also true of attempts to gain the privileges of those in high positions at work. They are only privileges as long as they are limited to a minority. If this view is a correct interpretation of the trend in patterns of expenditure an urgent review of objectives and the means of achieving them will be necessary if a mad and self-defeating frenzy with possibly alarming social consequences is to be avoided.

(h) The need for a critique of social projects. Another feature of social policy in modern society is the propensity to indulge in projects which turn out to be very expensive in resources: for example the creation of a public health service, a transport network or policies to regenerate inner cities. These projects cost a great deal and therefore need to be monitored very closely to avoid inefficiency. Moreover, the consequences of getting the policy wrong are very costly. An interesting example, from the Third World, is whether a developing country should go for a Western type medical service offering advanced medical services in the main cities or whether the same money should be used to set up a much more widespread, but also a more primitive, network of local medical services. What seems necessary is that modern society needs within it some sort of counter and critical activity which all the time provides the necessary radical evaluation of the major public and

[2] F. Hirsch, *The Limits to Social Growth,* Routledge and Keegan Paul 1977.

private trends. This is an area where many ecological groups have already proved their worth. Another important contribution is being made by such groups as those led by Ivan Illich[3] through their critical, and in a sense prophetic, analysis of social policies.

(i) Social planning and the individual. It appears that the more complex society becomes the more the concept of the individual and that of person is put under strain. We certainly seem to have reached a point where many people feel that they are forced to struggle to maintain their personal identity and their sense of individualism. As the Christian religion places the concept of person and the concept of personal salvation at the centre of its message, this is an area of considerable concern to the church. And as the object of true living is to give meaning to the concept of the whole man Christians must take a special interest in .trends which seem to be violating the concept of person. These trends also bring a timely reminder that the true nature of living also rests in the way in which it helps individuals to approach their God and emphasizes the snares in the delusion that social change in itself can bring about personal happiness and an attunement to God. On the other hand the Christian cannot support a defence of individualism as such. Our social obligations must be elevated to the highest point possible, often at the expense of self. Such an attitude is consistent with the church's interpretation of Christ as the Man for Others and provides a particularly pertinent understanding of the nature of man in the social debate at a time when the complexity of life poses acutely the conflict between social and indivdual needs.

The role of the church

What is the role of the Christian and the church in all this? The church is, or should be, the manifestation of Christ to the present generation and as such must seek to participate both corporately, and individually through the actions of individual Christians, in this process of defining and achieving a better society. This activity would above all be a sign that the church cares about people, cares about them both individually and socially and therefore cares about society as a whole. The church must not flinch, if necessary, from participating in the decision-making process. It is true that on many issues Christians will not have common views and therefore it would be pointless to try to provide a 'church' view. However, the one thing that Christians can share is a concern for the process of coming to decisions and the need for people to engage in debate and action

[3] See, for example, I. Illich, *Medical Nemesis,* Calder and Boyars 1975.

about the issues involved. The church should, therefore, actively encourage debate of the sort described earlier in the chapter and it will always, also, have a responsibility for putting before society the underlying moral principles which all of us must respect. There will be some issues where individual sections of the church, men with similar views, will want to take action and influence decisions. Where we agree with a group it is imperative that we join them and participate in this way. Even where we do not agree with a particular group's stance we must wish them God's blessing in whatever they are doing since their action will be part of the process of action and reaction which will clarify society's true course.

If the church is to be active in society in any sense it is essential that it should be an informed church. There is nothing worse than church pronouncements on social issues which so clearly have not taken into account all the various facets of the arguments. The ways in which the church can acquit itself properly in this way are many. They involve sometimes setting aside full-time staff to specialize in the study of economic, political and social aspects of society in order to enable the church to take a responsible view. Another way is through the church's own social work activities. Most denominations support specialist activities in the social work field (the National Children's Home, for example). Another way is through the work of the increasing number of ministers or priests engaged in full-time secular appointments. But the most important contribution must come from the layman, who, by definition, is wholly committed to the work of God in society and who has an essential experience to feed back into the thinking of the church generally on social and political issues. It is a pity that both, at national and local level, churches on the whole have yet to find a way of fully harnessing the experience and enthusiasm of their laity in framing Christian views on contemporary issues and the application of such views in practice. With these various channels open to them there is no excuse for churches not to be fully informed on the issues on which its members, individually or corporately, seek to involve themselves.

Of course the church must never forget its supportive role; to offer help, encouragement and spiritual nourishment to its members as they struggle in the day-to-day activities of society. The church exists to give depth and meaning to daily life and to provide resources which church members can draw on in order to face up to the daily life around them. There is no shame in church members turning their back for a while on what is going on around them in order to recharge themselves and no need to have to apologize for wanting time to think about the wider dimensions of life before returning to the fray.

Finally, the church must always be a prophetic church. While it goes without saying that the Christian activity of the day-to-day involvement of lay people makes a substantial contribution to society, there still remains the task of the church to be ready in one way or another to pass judgement on contemporary society as it has been required to do over each other society in the past. There comes a point where the church must say 'In the name of God . . .' and go on to condemn the iniquities of the age and call people to return to God. This is the vital role of the church and yet it has to be exercised without any loss of the sense of solidarity with man in society. The church must enable man to find his humanity while being ready at the appropriate time to declare the supremacy of God.

Although a contribution to prophecy comes in part from the layman in his daily life the main burden falls on the ordained ministry or on the church as an institution. The spur to, and the framing of, the prophetic intervention may be determined by the natural intercourse between ministers (priests) and the laity but there comes a point where the 'church' has to 'speak' to society and do so by disassociating itself, in a vital sense, from the loyalty of its laity to secular society.

There is a point of view that argues that this is a recipe for disaster. How can we expect the ordained ministry, so innocent and so unskilled in the ways of the world, to find the right thing to say, at the right time, about very often complex political/sociological issues? We are in the age of the specialist professional and there is no place for the over-enthusiastic and unskilled amateur. But this is a misunderstanding of the role and nature of prophecy. In the first place, quite often the prophetic voice is deceptively foolish. There is plenty of evidence in the Gospels for the view that the acceptance of God's will lead to the overturning of conventional ideas, of setting things on their heads. The kingdom of God is a place where the meek are respected and not the strong; where the last come first and where the poor and not the rich are blessed. There is nothing wrong, therefore, in anticipating that the prophetic word to our present day will appear bizarre and perhaps absurd. One of the essential features of protest is often its superficial futility. People chaining themselves to iron railings or marching through London in grotesque costume in one sense achieve nothing. Also the prophet who gets up and says 'I may not understand the complex financial situation and the rights and wrongs of the various cases under dispute at the moment, but it seems to me in the name of God that any system that has resulted in the present situation must be wrong' invites ridicule from those 'in the know'. And yet there is an essential case for this type of intervention and the saints of the past bear witness to it throughout the history of the church.

The ultimate protestor in this vein has always been the clown, the jester, the fool. He is the man who sees that the king has nothing on and makes people laugh about it. They laugh because the truth revealed by the clown's actions is too much to take seriously. I cannot speak too strongly in defence of this role of the church; this, as it were, nonsensical ability to penetrate through humanity's barriers, making people aware, through the absurd, of the absurdity of their own situation.

Of course, the prophetic voice will not be listened to. It will be rejected by all reasonable men. We will say that it is uninformed. How can the church claim a right to say anything about the current economic situation which even economists cannot understand? We will claim that the church is being disloyal. What a thing to do at a time of national crisis, actually to suggest that what the government, or some other pressure group, is doing may be wrong! We will say that the church is being unsympathetic. If only church leaders understood how difficult the situation was, how hard we were trying to get it right! The very least they should do is to offer us the sympathy of silence and encourage us to do our best! That would be far better than making an open issue of it. Here we are in a delicate position just about to get things right (we are always *about* to do) and the church intervenes with an extraordinary statement about the wrongness of the situation which has knocked another ten cents off the exchange rate! This whole attitude is, of course, summed up in the common cry of politicians and other leaders for the church to mind its own business and to keep out of current affairs. But unless the church plays this role, that of the layman in his compromise situations will mean nothing.

Does the consumer goods society contain any less grounds for hope than any other society in history? I doubt it. The characteristics of our society are vastly different from those of the past and there are alarming aspects of it, the worst being the intensive preoccupation of materialism of modern man and his wilful, wasteful consumption of resources. These dangers, however, can be matched with examples from other societies and other ages equally indicative of man's proneness to fail. What we have is a set of conditions which currently form the framework of daily life which in themselves are neither more nor less conducive to sin than any others. The church's task, as ever, is to distil from the contemporary situation the basic issues of right and wrong and to provide a sense of direction to be followed to achieve a better society. It is an awesome task but one in which the Christian will do grave disservice to his fellow men if he takes fright and tries to turn his back on it.

11 The challenge—personal commitment

For a Christian a book about modern living can only end with a challenge, to him as an individual, to assess his life-style in contemporary society. When the arguments have been deployed and the issues raised, we are left with the fact that each Christian awakes on each day and engages himself, in one form or another, with varying degrees of commitment, in the daily business of life. It is a life made up of both great things relating to the nature of society and the purpose of life itself, and little things concerning daily conduct in whatever situation he finds himself. That life requires an appraisal of each of an infinite number of actions and situations and demands a personal decision whether they are, or are not, to be dedicated to the glory of God.

The choice of role for the Christian

Underlying the Christian's attitude to these things, great and small, is a view about his life-style and it would make matters easy if there was a clear and unambiguous indication in his religion of the role he should adopt. Unfortunately this is not the case. The contemporary Christian has a variety of alternatives to choose from, some of which at first sight seem to be incompatible with others.

(a) The passive role. For many Christians nowadays the most congenial role is that of a servant of others. This view has strong biblical foundations, particularly in the Old Testament, and is particularly attractive to a Christian who wants to know how to live in a world which contains many distasteful characteristics such as the emphasis given to power, ambition and prestige and where Western Christians, particularly, find themselves so well endowed in material possessions. There is a basic sense of humility in this attitude of servant to others, which not only seems to be close to the image of Christ, but when practised often results in an opening up of situations and breaking down of barriers; the sort of liberating influence required in the world.

One problem, however, with this view is that the position of powerlessness associated with it has to be reconciled with the desire to affect change (which implies some influence, power, over the means of achieving change). Also in practice it turns out to be a difficult role for the Western Christian in relation to the development problem since he cannot wholly disassociate himself from the position of power arising out of his living in the richer part of the world. Whether he likes it or not, he operates from a privileged position.

There is, secondly, the attitude of what one may call, without offence I hope, the 'drop out' type of Christian. There are many Christians, an increasing number perhaps, who genuinely feel now that attempts, which Christians have often shared, to carry out social engineering, to create a better society, have abjectly failed and that the best working assumption to make is that all power systems are inherently bad and corrupting and invariably protect the privileged at the expense of the underprivileged. In the circumstances, they feel, it is better to attempt to exist with as little dependence on the system as possible. Modern groups of this persuasion are particularly offended by the wastefulness and potential to pollute of the industrial machine around them. This view is very basic and deserves to be taken much more seriously by a Christian than perhaps his secular contemporaries would wish to do. It is a modern example of the Christian tradition of abandoning secular society entirely, the traditionally expressed sense of vocation, of being called, to give up wealth. The trouble with this life-style, however, is that it is often adopted still withing the framework of a society which is sustained by the affluence and acquisitiveness of others. It would be fairer to compare living in the present society with life in one in which none of the more desirable benefits exist, e.g. where hospitals, schools and the social interstructure which we now take for granted, were missing.

Another view of role which was developed earlier[1] is linked closely with prophecy. There has always been a strong belief in the role of religion in bringing people to their senses and reminding them when they were seriously diverging from God's will. Although it is often regarded as a somewhat negative attitude of religion to cry 'woe' from time to time, a realistic view of our nature makes it clear that a robust challenge of this sort is necessary every so often if we are to be made aware of how wildly wrong we have been. The previous chapter discussed the role of the church itself in this respect and argued that at all times, and never more than now, it has been necessary for the church to execute a prophetic role. The question now is the part to be played by the Christian layman in relation to this role of the church. The church is never welcome when it feels impelled to prophesy in this way and people, and that includes Christians as well as non-Christians, invariably resent it when it is done. The traditional reactions are to criticize the church for finding

[1] See Chapters 4 and 10.

the wrong moment to say what it wants to, to criticize it for being uninformed about secular matters in which it has no standing, or criticize it for being idealistic and not being sympathetic enough to others who are trying to achieve the best they possibly can in a very difficult situation. Christian laymen engaged in secular life will invariably be in the forefront of putting these questions back to the church, which paradoxically they love and serve.

As we have noted earlier the true prophetic voice often seems to come through in odd occasions and though odd characters. Sometimes the very strength of the prophetic voice lies in its absurdity. It is often the fruitless gesture, seemingly uninformed observation about events, which although denied at the time, penetrates to the heart of the matter; to repeat, it is very much the case of the little boy seeing the king in his birthday suit when others cannot.

One of the self-denying ordinances that the lay Christian must, therefore, accept, at whatever level of power he operates in his society, is to listen to the words of the innocent. They are all the more important to listen to by virtue of the fact that they are innocent and unimportant, since it is often quite clear where the informed and less innocent line of reasoning is taking us! A Christian has a difficult task coming to terms with this, his dual responsibility. As we have seen earlier, on the one hand, he is committed to his secular organization in every respect while on the other he is well and truly part of that church which in its wisdom and in its good time will stand up and condemn what is being done by the very institutions which the layman serves. Perhaps the most useful definition of a layman is that one who is hired by and works for a secular institution which commands his complete loyalty and who therefore at crucial points of judgement has to stand ready to be judged rather than to judge.[2]

(b) The active role. In contrast to this group of, as it were, more passive Christian roles, there are a number which are far more active and participatory in society. For example, a role often adopted by Christians is that of being, so to speak, the responsible citizen. Christians on the whole are against tyranny, anarchy, indifference and disorder and therefore are strongly tempted to support preservative elements in society such as a good government, law and order and a well-disciplined democratic process such as has developed in Britain. Democracy seems to offer the most efficient means of reconciling differences between citizens and pressure groups without the urge to hate and the oppression that seems to

[2] If developed, this definition helps to provide an equally useful definition of a minister or priest.

appear in other types of systems. The Christian is thus influenced in the way in which he behaves in society by his desire to make it work. He wishes to play a useful and, if possible, prominent part in the processes of such a society and wants to be involved in local or national politics or through other power centres. So the Christian is led not only to strive for responsible leadership and for positions of power within the existing system, but also to take up a defensive and protective attitude to the institutions he has helped to create. The attractions of this approach are many and appeal particularly to those who believe in social engineering and want to improve society. The dangers are equally obvious. The attitude encourages Christians to defend a particular type of privilege and power. They have to be very sure in themselves that the type of power structure they have committed themselves to is the right one, if they are to be wedded to its defence.

Another view closely related to the previous one is what may be termed the 'powerhouse' view of Christian involvement. The argument for this approach runs along the following lines. Christians should be involved in society and have views about where society should go. Therefore the more Christians can influence decisions to achieve their objectives the better. This leads to the view that Christian leaders are a good thing and that influence by Christians on leaders is a good thing. It is a very elitist view of society and of Christian action. For these reasons it may be a very unhappy view for many Christians, particularly for those who are inclined to prefer the model of the servant, and yet its logic cannot be denied. It is very difficult not to feel pleased and comforted when one reads that the President of the United States is a practising Christian, or that this or that trade union leader in this country is a committed Christian. Similarly, for example, the Christian can derive satisfaction when the church is invited to give evidence to a Royal Commission about major social questions and its views are given more prominence than in past years.

It is also a factor affecting Christian personal life since a similar argument is often used to justify personal ambition for a Christian. That is to say, while the Christian might argue that he wishes to work for the good of society and is not interested in personal ambition he could say that the higher the position he achieves the greater his potential for good on behalf of others. Thus he can justify his attempts to be promoted or to get into positions of power. Of course, the dangers of such an attitude are very obvious. To put it bluntly we have no evidence at all that Jesus sought to achieve status or power in this sense in the community of his time. It is true that by the time of the Emperor Constantine the joint powers of church and state were blended together, but scholars now detect a distinct change in the tenor and nature of the church's message and teaching subsequent to that event which was not there in the early primitive church. One wonders whether it was the church that took over the state or the state took over the church at that moment. Recent studies in Christian origins have, by searching the early records to understand what the real early Christian community was all about, unravelled very many disturbing facets of community life which if applied now would cause many Christians much unease and embarrassment.

A further extension of this argument is the attitude of those who broadly argue that as Christians they should 'stay in the kitchen'. The argument is that at the end of the day progress towards the kingdom of God will be seen through the actions of society and the direction in which it moves. This means that the social and political game is something that Christians must play because if they are not there taking decisions others who have different ideals and different objectives will take their place. It is essential, therefore, runs the argument, to be involved in the decision-making process to achieve the best possible world. There is an ancillary, personal, argument supporting this view which is that Christian living consists of taking decisions for or against God in the world and not in contemplation or isolation from the world. The more the Christian is involved in day-to-day affairs, therefore the more he will have the opportunity to be tested whether he is for or against God.

To put it mildly, it is not at all clear how these differing views of the role of the Christian in society can be reconciled. The foregoing paragraphs have shown that there are views ranging from a strong interventionist and activist view at one end, to an equally coherent and cogent set of arguments leading to an inequivocal withdrawal and rejection of society's values at the other. In favour of the interventionist's view are the arguments that the Christian should be a responsible citizen, that he should seek to achieve as much power as he can in order to influence events and that it is necessary both for society's sake and for his own salvation that he should be engaged in the decision-making process of everyday life. On the other side the withdrawal symptoms, as it were, are the need for the Christian to be set in the role of a servant, the need to disengage from all the bad aspects of materialistic society, to seek a new style of life and the need to enable the true prophetic voice to be uttered at the appropriate time.

Our personal experience must, and actually does, contain in it tendencies in each of these directions which are best seen in terms of a dialectic. We want to improve society but beware of the temptations of power, praise, reward and self-aggrandizement! We want to concentrate on a search for God through contemplation but remember the judgement prepared for those who fail to help their neighbour! We have no desire for a leadership role and yet there are occasions when only we seem in a position to provide it! We can sense the thrill of winning a particular political battle but we must balance carefully what we will really win and what we might lose in the battle! Those that seek to choose between the two extremes are, therefore, probably doomed to failure. The mixture of roles represents one of the vital paradoxes of life—a divinely created tension.

The conduct of daily life

The preceding section has been concerned with the question of the Christian's individual role in contemporary society. There is a second task which is to suggest ways in which the Christian should conduct his daily life in the context of economic activity. Preceding chapters have attempted to show the sense of unity underlying the concepts of *man the producer* or *man the consumer*, both of which ultimately come back to a view about the nature of man himself. For a moment now it will help to disentangle the two concepts once more and consider first of all some points of view about man the producer.

As has been said earlier, the concept has been central to the church's views about man and work. We are only just emerging out of a period when the struggle to survive has dominated most people's lives into a period when people in general can afford the thought of what to do with time other than use it for providing the basic necessities of life. We are now able to lay bare what might in retrospect turn out to have been a coincidence, in which it was not necessary to differentiate between the need for man to work to keep himself alive and the need for man to work as a desirable activity. If we can now ignore the task of providing necessities for survival it becomes a very interesting question as to what we think God's will for us really is in terms of work? Are we supposed to strive for a sun-lounge society in which we do nothing but laze around all day? Or are we to assume that we must continue to do things, let us say making products, because there is some primeval urge to carry on in this way? Or are we going to say that although man is destined always to be active it is the Christian task to make sure that such activity is channelled into good works and things for the benefit of society? It is regrettable that this issue of the reason for effort and activity and the respective values of not doing things as distinct from doing things, and where the activity of thinking and reflection enters into a view of life, has been grossly neglected as an area of study by Christian thinkers. Without such study we cannot be sure what is the true nature and destiny of man in this modern affluent society. For example, if we assume that man is content, say, with his present standard of living, would he be willing to spend the rest of his time (other than that engaged in maintaining his present standard of living) in voluntary activity? Or must he work for money? The obvious answer is that money should not matter, but we know that many people prefer to do paid rather than voluntary work simply because money matters not in the sense of providing them with extra income, but by representing the value that society puts on their activities. It is by no means obvious that voluntary work is more desirable than paid work in a structure provided by a professional organization. But this simply serves to underline the fact that we know very little about our motivations for various forms of activity, particularly in the altruistic field.

To take another example: the question of leisure. It is easy to say that it is a good thing for people to have more leisure and that that leisure should be put to good purposes in the interest of the community. But what do we mean by increased leisure? Do we mean the taking of holidays? Do we mean participation in, say, local government? Do we mean the running of youth clubs? All of these involve activity of one sort or another and many of them involve decision-making and situations involving personal relationships which are very similar to those found in the typical working environment. Where do we look to measure the blessing of leisure? Is it in terms of satisfaction given to the individuals participating in leisure, or is it in their contribution to the goals of society? Have we some view that the quality of social engineering will be in a sense better if it is brought about by voluntary 'leisure time' activities than if it is done through a professional system such as, for example, local authority social welfare or amenity services? Maybe there is more to be said for the voluntary case but it is an area which needs to be explored much more thoroughly by experts before we start forming a policy for the future.[3]

This brings us back to the need to disentangle man the producer in the sense of work being required to provide necessities and man the producer in the sense that work is an activity, and a necessary activity, in which man achieves himself in the fullest possible sense. Perhaps participation in the productive process, either on the

[3] See, for example, David Bridge, *Looking at Leisure,* Epworth Press 1978.

factory floor, in offices, in high or low positions of leadership, matters not simply because we are part of a process producing goods and services but much more so in the sense that these activities provide the forum, the cockpit as it were, in which we live out our daily lives, find out who we are as persons and learn to relate to others both in times of good and bad relationships and in times of success and failure. This is the stuff of living and the moulding of our true self out of all these times of frustration and challenge is a much greater Christian objective than the speed, orientation or whatever else of economic growth and the state of the industrial machine. Can we conceive of a situation in which man is not challenged in these terms to fulfil his ambition? Has the Christian any better alternative to offer in which man can achieve his potential? Has the Christian an alternative view of a social environment in which man could better go through this process of growing up and maturing? I would like to think he has, but it has yet to be formulated rigorously and until it is an essential element in the Christian critique of present economic society will be missing.

The creation of our attitudes towards consumption and material possessions, i.e. to man the consumer, has to be approached in exactly the same way. Of course it matters how much we buy and consume, and what we buy and consume, and it matters acutely when there are millions in the world who are so short of purchasing power that they are about to die, and we must pray for a more Christian society in which these issues are more fairly thrashed out and resolved. But at the end of the day, those arguments are only about material things and views about possessions will make no sense unless we get behind them to identify their real importance to us as we strive for maturity. I have already acknowledged that I give a great deal of weight to the school of thought that sees these possessions and our relationships with others at work and in acts of consumption primarily as part of a communication network which is allowing, to a greater or lesser degree, individuals to achieve a sense of worth. That is what life appears to be all about and is the area in which we gauge whether we feel people are happier, are more dignified, are more mature and in Christian terms, more attuned to the purpose of God. The basic objective must be, therefore to enable people to realize what the whole mad rush of production and consumption is really all about and enable them to relate more maturely and more positively, with or without the help of material possessions, to their fellows and to God. This way we shall at least lay the groundwork for a society in which a true understanding of the desirability of the rate of economic growth and its direction can be assessed and we shall produce a calmer and more purposeful society.

A view of the mature man must contain in it a potential to respond to all the great claims imposed by God—to love our neighbour, to be stewards to his world—but it must also contain within that maturity a full opportunity for the exercise of our human drive and initiative. The latter often reveals itself in aggression, in acquisitiveness and power seeking, but there are sufficient examples, in the selfless dedication of great men, of explorers and martyrs, to show to what great purposes the restless drive of humanity can be turned, God willing. Maturity, in other words, is not necessarily a soft option made up of the humbler graces, the dignity of man also resides in a herioc view of his nature, in his strengths, ready to be channelled to meet the great challenges thrown out by nature and the growth of society.

A Christian concern about the modern materialistic and acquisitive society is thus not mainly a concern about the right use of resources or of attaining social goals, though of course it is that as well, but it is a question of searching for the deep underlying spiritual framework which man is seeking to express today via the materialistic and acquisitive society that we live in. If that primary problem is resolved or at least revealed, then we will begin to understand the nature of, as it were, the secondary problems. By recognizing the true spiritual challenge facing man in his attempt to achieve maturity there will be many things to be said about the way he should behave in terms of business practice, in terms of the conduct of affairs and his relationships with others but these answers must derive from a true understanding of underlying motivation. This line of thought comes full circle back to the distinction made earlier between individuals and persons. *Man the person* is a vital concept to the Christian, since it embodies in it the view that we are not individuals indulging in activities solely designed to maximize our own pleasure and, where concessions are made to others, only as a means of maximizing our own well-being. The concept of person places our relationship with others, our concern and care for others, and therefore our concern for society, on a level above self-interest; to a Christian the less of self and the more of others is the path to the kingdom of God. Relationships with others, the grounds on which we, in the main, seek to be obedient to the will of God, must be the dominant factor in our daily work, in our actions as consumers and, above all, in our role as citizens. It must be dominant because behind the charade of economic activity lies the far more serious task of living and dying—when, in each moment, we have the chance to enter the kingdom of heaven or not.

A close study of the recorded sayings of Jesus about involvement in the world around us leaves the conclusion that, on the whole, Jesus was neutral about many things that agitate us so much today. He did not tell us to take over the world's economic leadership. He did not tell us to get involved in the world around us. On the other hand our understanding of the teaching and ministry of Jesus makes it clear that there are many things, such as poverty and oppression, which the Christian must attack as best he can.

But the overriding impression is that these things did not matter because they were not the most important ones. The Gospel message is the demand that we be obedient to God in whatever we do. That means that the Christian must have a strategy lasting to eternity, if needs be, by which he seeks to be obedient to God and yet essentially that task is crucially focused on the decision of the moment. Decisions for or against God in each situation as it confronts us, are both consistent with our obedience to God in the long run and are crucial to our obedience to God as of now. We have to live every day ahead for God, indeed every minute for that matter. And this we have to do despite the fact that we must hope where often there are no grounds for doing so. We must continue to try to build Utopia when history is completely against us and where indeed in one sense we know we will not succeed. We must strive and seek to succeed in a way that appears to contradict much of the Christian view of the nature of man and which can only perhaps be justified by our love for others. Finally, we will be impelled by our faith to die, if needs be, for a world which in a very real sense does not matter.

Our daily decisions for or against God encapsulate all that is meant by the act of commitment to God. They embrace in one flash of the moment, our sense of repentance, our trust in God and our declaration of obedience to his will. Given this we can be content that all else will follow. And we can rest assured that much else will indeed follow, since from that alliance, in that moment, between the spirit of man and his God will flow a stream of imperatives for application in our daily lives—the application of love, the striving to build anew, to progress, at least a little, in human development. But above all, a true understanding of God's will for us in that very moment will lead to a true understanding of our relations with others. From the relationship with others will come a true understanding of how to build the new Jerusalem, an indication of the way in which God expects us to make use of this truly breathtaking opportunity opening out before us through our increasing control over nature.

The challenge—personal commitment

The Christian has today, as always, somehow to attempt to meet three challenges in the task of daily living. The first is to reconcile hope with reality. The second is to find the means of co-existence between a daily life of merit and value and an awareness of the appalling sense of failure in the persistence of the great human blasphemies, such as world poverty. The third is to learn how to grow into maturity with God and with our fellow man in both personal and social terms and through that maturity turn all that is at our disposal in this world to the glory of God.